Dearest Donna,

You make a great sister & sister in law. You do so much & care so much. Thank you for all that you do. Thank you for your support as well. May God bless you & give you your hearts desire.

Love
Norma Jean

Other books in **The Tin Train Series**
By Norma Jean

Book One – Ella's Children
Book Two – The North Wind
Book Three - 514

The Home

Book Four of

The Tin Train Series

By Norma Jean

Woodrow Wilson School

Denty Publications

Norma Jean author's page

http://www.amazon.com/Norma-Jean/e/B00I2A6130

Dedication

I would like to dedicate this book to all those that put out the extra effort to help the children that others have dubbed as unworthy, or difficult. This includes social workers, teachers, pastors, and anyone who has attempted to help a child in need. Even if the child did not respond in an obvious way, they knew and appreciated what you did for them.

Introduction

In book 3, I ended with the beginnings of a big family meeting. What do we do with the Baas children? They have become so unruly, according to the stepmother.

They had proof too! Didn't they?

The kids were sneaking in and out of the house all hours of the day and night. They were ascending and descending off the roof. They were climbing down to the banister and away they went.

There are only four of us now living in the house on Harris Avenue. One of the children was supposedly in Franklin Village, according to the stepmother. However, he wasn't really he had been staying with a relative of my dad's, one of our aunt's house. Another one of the children ran away.

So where do we go? Where do you put a family this large?

There were still six of my dad's children left to make a decision on. Where they should go to live? With whom should they live with?

Chapter 1

Debbie Dressed As An Old Woman

The next morning our house was still in an uproar. The stepmother was seething. I had never seen her so mad. None of us had ever seen her so mad and we had seen her mad on many occasions. Debbie had been gone for more than twenty-four hours now. Joan and I were happy. Elated actually was more the word that she (Debbie) had gotten away, at least someone had gotten away. Not a soul in the house got any sleep last night. When the stepmother was mad, she was yelling and screaming constantly at the top of her lungs, and that was pretty loud. The noise would go right through you and shatter every one of your nerve endings. It was one of those situations where you just start shaking all over, from your nerves. You know that feeling you get when you are so cold or so scared that you start quivering and shivering. This was one of those times.

That's how Joan and I felt. We were shaking so bad we could not stop. Sometimes, even as adults, we still start shaking uncontrollably when a memory is triggered. We were actually quivering from the top of our head to the tips of our toes, from our nerves being shattered.

Yes! Joan, Freddie and I, all three of us had gotten another beating last night, but someone escaped too. This was very exciting news to us. Daryl escaped the beatings this time. He was a little more on the reserved side, he didn't sneak out. I think he was too afraid of getting caught. Plus, he was tiny. He was too little to reach the banister from the roof.

The morning after Debbie sneaked out of the house. Debbie's friends could see she was quite serious about staying away from our house on Harris Avenue. She was not going to go back, ever. If they made her go back, she would just run away again. Debbie had the elation of knowing it was possible now. We knew that she was done with Harris Avenue and we were glad for her! Joan and I were cheering her on all the way, silently though, so no one would know. We were all waiting for our chance to escape.

Debbie's friends helped her to get away, finally. They did not force her to go back to our house with our stepmother. She was ready to walk all the way to Grandma Lamb's house if she had to. We knew how to get there. We had walked to grandma's house many times. These people decided to help her get to grandma's house. They did not waste any more time in doing so.

It took some doing because the stepmother was still scouring the neighborhood looking for Debbie. She knew in her heart if the authorities found out what she had been doing to her step children she would be in trouble. She knew she would lose us all of us, including her own children.

Grandma Lamb did not waste time after Debbie got to her house either. She knew time was of the essence. She knew that our stepmother was a conniving, wicked woman. Grandma also knew that things could go wrong if things were not handled properly with the authorities.

She disguised Debbie as an old woman. Then grandma took Debbie to children's services. Grandma Lamb was a very small woman so her clothes fit Debbie perfectly. Both grandma and Debbie were four feet nine and a half or four foot ten inches tall. It worked to disguise Debbie this way. They were about the same size. Grandma had white hair, she put an old woman's scarf on Debbie's head.

Unfortunately, at this time, unless there was an adult who was an eyewitness, to these horrendous crimes perpetrated against these children there was nothing that children's services could do. There was nothing more the authorities could do to help these children. Their hands were tied. Luckily, for us, our sister Karen had moved back to Columbus. She had seen firsthand all the beatings, the whippings, and things. Karen was an adult.

Grandma called Karen to come to children's services. Grandma explained to Karen what the situation was and how critical it was for her to get there as quick as possible. Time was of the essence. This was to keep everyone off guard. So Karen got to children's services as quick as she could. Karen's nerves were a mess and shattered as well. She spent four years with the woman herself. She grew up in the same household as the rest of us. It takes a long time for one to get over these things, if you ever do. Karen did not waste any time getting to children's services. Karen explained how bad the situation on Harris Avenue really was. She described in full detail, the beatings we received and what they beat us with. Karen described how they had taken a hose one inch in diameter and spliced it in four's all the way down to a handle. This made it flexible and with a grip to hold on to. The hose cut this way stuck to the skin, cut and bruised the skin too.

The beatings were horrific. She told them they were not light taps either they were a full-blown beating. She told the caseworker that these beatings were so bad they left the kids bleeding, with bruises, and welts and numb on most of the skin surfaces. As Karen went on to describe in detail the crimes committed against us as children the caseworker was writing up his case against the stepmother.

Karen described how we were locked in the basement, whenever the mood struck our stepmother. She described how the kids could not go out and play during the summertime. In the winter, they had to stay outside all day long and could not even go inside for a bathroom break. She described how the windows in the second story of our house were nailed shut and painted so that no air could circulate, even in the summertime. She finally described how we would be forced to eat food that had sat out all night and all day the next day and we got food poisoning from this food. The caseworker just shook his head he could not believe what he was hearing.

With this knowledge, they were able to proceed with the case at hand. They immediately made us wards of the state of Ohio.

Thank God, Karen listened to her gut instinct.

God had told Karen, she was needed here in Columbus to help protect her brothers and sisters from this woman. She immediately left New Hampshire where she was living at the time. I do not know how she convinced her husband she wanted or needed to move back or had to move back. She listened to what God was telling her. Thank God for the sixth senses or as some would say the gut instinct, He gives us.

She had to convince her husband that she needed and wanted to move back to Ohio. She could not tell him that God told her she was needed back in Ohio. He would have thought she was out of her mind. Karen did convince her husband she was needed here in Columbus. They packed everything up and moved back here, just in the nick of time.

He found a good job at Rickenbacker. So he was more than happy to oblige. God did have a hand in it.

Karen came back here to live. She knew God was going to tell her, what needed to be done once she was back here. God did let her know too. She let her instinct take control.

We don't always listen to what God is telling us but this time Karen did.

The caseworker called together a big family meeting. All the kids (those that were still living in our house) and those children living with other family members were ordered to participate. This was not a minor invitation, this was a command performance, they were told to be there.

All the members of our family were told to come to this meeting, including both of our grandma's. All the older brothers and sisters who lived in Columbus were told to come. They received a personal phone call.

I do not know how such a meeting was ordered, so quickly but this caseworker managed the impossible.

Chapter 2

Big Family Meeting - Adults Only

The doorbell rang!

The stepmother answered the door. Grandma Lamb was there, Debbie was there, the caseworker was there as well. Oh! How the stepmother hated Grandma Lamb.

The caseworker got right to the point, for the purpose of this meeting. He had an adult eyewitness to the abuses going on in this house. He was here to find the underlying cause of these allegations.

We lived with our stepmother for one year without our dad. No one tried to come and get us from this woman. They all knew what she was like; they had all seen her in action. She was evil incarnate. We were only trying to protect each other and ourselves from the onslaught of evil from this woman. No one seemed to care.

I still to this day do not understand why our relatives let us stay in this situation for so long, after our dad died. It was bad enough with our dad being the way he was. Grandma being the way she was, she was very scary. They all knew this woman was worse than grandma and dad ever were and they were pretty bad. Grandma Lamb knew she was worse. Karen knew she was worse. She too lived with the woman.

Junior had seen her in action many times but he seemed oblivious to everything the stepmother was doing. Grandma Baas never cared for us so she had not changed any. I did not expect her to either.

Why did they not come to our rescue?

Some of them had good reasons. Larry was in boot camp. John too was in boot camp. Neither one of them could come to the rescue. Vera was also in the military, so she could not help us either.

The whole family had a court order to show up to a family meeting. This meeting was held at our house on Harris Avenue where we had been living. Grandma Baas was there. Junior and his wife were there. The stepmother was there. Grandma Lamb was there with Debbie in tow.

Oh! If looks could kill, Debbie would have been dead with the look of pure hatred, the stepmother had on her face. The veins on her face and neck were just popping out all over. Her face was red, and it was tense. Her voice was terse. (This happened when she was mad her veins would be popping.) Her lips were a solid thin line.

The caseworker started asking questions about what should happen to all of us kids. He got right to the point. He did not mince words. All of us kids had to be there too. Jimmy came back for this special occasion. Supposedly, he was at Franklin Village, but we found out later, much later he had spent the whole summer with one of our aunts. The stepmother told Alan, to tell Karen, she could not come to these proceedings. Karen did not know she could over rule her husband. We had been so battered as children, it took us a long time to stand up for ourselves as adults, some still do not stick up for themselves.

Grandma Baas spoke up and said, "They could always go to an orphanage." Grandpa Baas did not come. He felt we should stay together but he did not care enough to come. In this, he did not get a say. Junior and his wife picked grandma Baas up because she did not drive.

Grandma Lamb said, "Over my dead body."

Grandma Baas said, "That can be arranged" as she laughed at her own joke. The two grandmas' never did get along. Grandma Baas thought she could do no wrong. When our mother died, she had wanted us to go an orphanage than. (Grandma Baas had never liked our mother so she in turn never liked us either.) Grandma Lamb would not even think of that possibility. The caseworker looked around the room at all these people gathered together in this room and he could not believe that they felt this was the best option. He even said as much. He could not believe the animosity going on either.

I was seventeen. The caseworker thought I was old enough to sit in on these proceedings. Therefore, I did. The stepmother did not like this one bit. She said, "Over my dead body. Norma has no business staying here for these proceedings." I was tired of being forced to doing something I did not want to do. All my life up to this point they said, "Norma do this." Norma did that. "Norma fetch me this or get me that." I fetched it. There was very little that I did not do, that I was told to do. At this point, I was not going to listen to my stepmother. God had finally broken the spell. He wanted me to snap out of the fog I had been in. He was about to give us the freedom that I and my brothers and sisters needed to escape. We were going to go. I could feel it in my bones. I was not going to let someone else make the decision for us.

The caseworker said I could stay for the adult meeting. He said, "You are old enough." There is that look again, that murderous look, from the stepmother. I was shaking in my skin. I was shaking that uncontrollable shaking you get when you are cold. It was summertime. I was not cold, at least not temperature cold. This shaking was from a deep seeded fear. Nevertheless, I stayed. I knew this meeting would affect me and my brothers and sisters for the rest of our lives. I felt it in my gut this was my duty. No one was going to make this decision of where we were going to live without my help. Not if I could help it.

I was tired of the abuse I was getting. I was tired of all the abuse my brothers and sisters were getting too. I was tired of all the beatings.

The caseworker looked at my stepmother and asked her, "What has brought things to such an impasse?"

The stepmother said, "These kids do nothing but resist me at every turn. I can no longer control them. They disobey all my orders. They are disrespectful. They are completely out of control. They have completely destroyed my house and everything in it."

The caseworker said, "What do you suggest I do with them."

The stepmother spoke up and said, "Put them in an institution would be my recommendation. Like their grandmother Baas, thinks should happen. Obviously they do not want to be here or they would not have sneaked out and run away."

The caseworker said, "Well that is two votes for going someplace else."

The caseworker said, "What about you Mrs. Lamb, what do you think should happen to them."

Grandma said, "I will take them. They can live with me. They did it once they can do it again."

He said, "What about John? I have heard he has been having sexual relations with the girls."

Grandma Lamb said, "Well boys will be boys, they have to have their play things."

The caseworker just shook his head. He could not believe what he was hearing. He began that writing thing he does. He was making notes and making quotations before he finally spoke again.

The caseworker said, "Well what about you, Art? What do you think should happen to your brothers and sisters?" I was not used to my brother Junior being called Art. In family settings, but then I remembered that this person (the caseworker) did not know that and this was not a normal family setting. He called Junior by his given name.

Junior said, "Well if John is any example of how the rest of the kids are, then they cannot come to live with us. We have two young children of our own to consider. I do not think it would work out for us to take them in.

The caseworker said; "Now I need some privacy to talk with Norma and her siblings."

The stepmother said, "How dare you, to be so presumptuous in my house. This does not concern these brats and that is all they are. They are lying conniving brats."

The caseworker said, "This does not concern you mam. You may leave the room as well."

The stepmother stomped out of the room! That is how mad she was. As soon as the stepmother left the room, the caseworker did not waste any time asking me questions. He said, "You know Norma you do not have to go."

I said, "Yes I do. My brothers and sisters need me. They look up to me. I have always taken care of them. If they go, I go. It will make it easier on them. Where they go I go."

He said, "Okay kids pack up your things and let's go."

The stepmother said, "No! I will do it. Get them out of my house and get them out now. Get them out of my sight. I cannot even stand to look at them one moment longer." The stepmother had been listening in around the corner. I should have been prepared for this outburst but I was not.

If my knees were not knocking before they were now. If the stepmother could have smacked us without getting into trouble she would have. She was deadly serious about getting us out of this house.

That is exactly what happened we left that very minute.

But, first things first, the caseworker needed to have a talk with all us kids first before we could leave.

.

Chapter 3

Big Family Meeting - Kids Only

Before the caseworker or anyone else left, he had to have a talk with all of us kids, after the adult meeting. He wanted to see what we thought as well. It was part of his job to see for himself how bad the situation truly was and report back to his superior's. He knew that whatever happened today was going to affect us kids for the rest of our lives.

He was a very small black man. He exuded energy and walked with a lot of confidence, stemming from welding power over bullying abusers. He was around five feet three inches tall. His hair was cut close to his head. He weighed around one hundred and twenty five pounds. He was a quiet man. When he spoke you listened! He did not say much. He asked a lot of questions. He kept writing things down on his tablet. He wore glasses, which he kept shoving on his nose. The heat of the day made the bridge of his nose slippery. So they kept sliding down, but he never missed a beat.

He seemed like a nice man. We already did not trust adults so this was no exception. A lot of adults said, "They were interested in us." However, no one wanted to follow through and help us. No one wanted to get involved.

All the adults were told to leave the proceedings. The caseworker asked us what we thought. He asked us all, "What do you think should happen to you." We all said we did not know. We were not used to adults asking us our opinion. Most adults treated us with disdain or an object not as a person. They treated us as though we did not have a mind to articulate a sentence. They definitely did not want to have a conversation with any of us.

Then he talked to us individually. He asked, "What do you think should happen to you? The way I see it you have two choices; one is to go to a relative's house, the second choice is for you all to go to an orphanage.

I told him, "Grandma Baas does not want us. She never has wanted us. She is too old even if she did want us. Junior is too young. Vera is too young. Karen is too young. Grandma Lamb was too old, so I guess it is to the orphanage we go. I also told him I could not stand one more night in this place. I told him that I not stand another one of my brothers or sisters to get another beating, like Freddie and Joan got yesterday."

He told me, "I didn't have to go I could stay right here and finish High School, it was my senior year."

What did this caseworker think that I was too old for a beating? Is he crazy? Not one of us was immune to the beatings in this place. Not one of us was immune to the abuse going on in this house. None of us was immune to it. I told him, "I needed to go because my sisters and brothers needed me to go with them." I also needed to go because I had always protected them. Well not very well, as it turns out. I too was only a child. I loved them as if they were my own children. I needed to go for me. I needed to make sure they were going to be ok. I needed to see that things were going to be ok.

How bad could this place be? We had already been through so many traumas. How much worse could our lives get after all this?

I told the caseworker I said, "I did not have friends in High School. I was not allowed to participate in any activities in High School where I could have met friends. So what do I have to stay here for, more abuse?"

I was always too busy taking care of family. I was always too busy working, to help bring in extra money.

When you are in an abusive situation, you cling to each other. You do not let outsiders in. You are not allowed to let others in. Your family is your friends. This is the way our family was. Yes, it was almost to the point of being sick in itself. The way we clung to each other but this is all we knew. This is all we had. We only had each other. We could not trust adults. The adults had already shown they could not be trusted. Occasionally we would catch a glimpse of what loving families could be like.

It seemed like the caseworker was there a long time. He was there at the house most of the day.

I think the caseworker knew we were serious.

That very day we left, lock stock and barrel. We were not allowed to go to our rooms and get our things. The stepmother just wanted us gone. The stepmother said, "Get out! Get out of my house now!" She is screaming this at the top of her lungs. She said, "I will pack up what is yours and have someone bring them to you. You will leave my house now this very minute."

I could not believe the caseworker let the stepmother speak to him this way but he did. He did not say a word to her. I am surprised the caseworker did not get the police involved so that we could at least get our clothes. He did not. We should have been allowed to get our stuff. We were not allowed to take anything that was ours with us. Not that we had that much but it was ours.

We left with only the clothes on our back. We did not have a change of underwear; or a change of socks; or a change of clothes. Truth was we probably were not wearing any socks. In the summertime, socks were a premium too expensive. We could not even take any personal items like hairbrushes or toothbrushes. We didn't have personal items anyway. However, if we had, we would not have been allowed to take them with us. There wasn't anything in this house that belonged to us anymore. The stepmother was going to make sure we left with nothing and we did. We left with nothing!

The stepmother's kids were not at home. They had gone to stay with someone so they were not around at the time all this was going on. We did not know where they had gone. We never were allowed to say good-bye to them. We were sad about this. We lived with them for six years. We were really friendly with some of them. The stepmother blamed us for all the problems. It was not our fault. We were just kids. We were just kids trying to live like normal kids would live.

The stepmother said that she would pack up our things and have them ready for us. Ready for what, was what I was thinking.

We went to Grandma Lamb's house. When school started grandma enrolled us in school. I think grandma was hoping that the orphanage would never materialize. I think most of us were hoping the orphanage would never materialize.

By this time, we still did not have any of our clothes from Harris Avenue. The stepmother had not sent them to us nor had she called and told us they were ready.

Grandma had to buy us clothes, before we could start school. I felt this was an unreasonable thing for our stepmother to do. She should have sent our clothes to us right away. She knew grandma could not afford to buy us clothes. Our clothes were not much anyway. They were ours though. They were the only thing we had. She knew grandma could not afford make ends meet. She also knew the burden of financing clothes for her grandchildren would be hardship for her.

The stepmother didn't care. The stepmother and Grandma Lamb had never seen eye to eye about anything. This cavalier attitude was just another fine example. Grandma Baas never visited us once when we were at Grandma Lamb's this summer.

Chapter 4

Back With Grandma

The caseworker along with Grandma Lamb's help took us to our grandma's house. This was to be a temporary arrangement until the orphanage had our papers ready. The caseworker said so. It also took some preparations to get things ready for us. There were six of us to get ready. We were all thinking and hoping this may have been permanent, staying with grandma because it was something we knew. Grandma had thought about hiring a lawyer to get custody of us. The lawyer told her it would cost her more than she could afford and it may still not do her any good. He said, "You may spend all that money and still loose custody of your grandchildren. I wouldn't recommend it."

During this time grandma enrolled us in school. We had been there that long. School had started. I think grandma was praying we would get to stay with her. I think she was still fighting to get custody of us. She just couldn't believe that the authorities would think an institution was a better alternative than living with her would be. The stepmother kept us because of the money she received from the government.

Since no one had taken us in after our dad died, it was too late to worry about that now. They had all left us with our stepmother. This in the eyes of the law said, "She (the stepmother) must not be that bad of a person since no one else wanted to take these children into their home." She was already telling lies about us. She said, "My stepchildren were destroying my house." The house was in our name. Dad left it to his children. Besides when you had fifteen kids living in a house, it is going to look worn and tired. There will be handprints on the wall. The linoleum and carpet will look worn and thread bare, with tread marks everywhere.

She had forced us to sign over powers of attorneys for all of our possessions, shortly after our dad died. Debbie had read the papers before she was prevented from doing so. The stepmother prevented any of the rest of us from seeing what we were signing. Debbie was asking why she had to do this. This made her, the stepmother, mad. This made Debbie mad too. Debbie was fed up with people taking stuff that was not theirs to take. The stepmother just made the rest of us sign our name to a piece of paper. She covered up the writing so that the rest of us could not read it. Later on, we found out that this was how she was able to empty all of our savings accounts. Both Jimmy and I had savings accounts worth well over a thousand dollars each. The power of attorney also gave her custody of our house. That was how she was able to take possession of the house on Harris Avenue, which was in our name.

Grandma had not changed one bit. She was still mean and feisty as ever. She was still hollering at us all the time. She was still hitting us in the face at every chance she got.

One would have thought since she had not seen us in a while she would have been glad to see us. Oh! She was glad to see us but she wanted to make sure we did not make waves. She did not want us causing trouble. By now all six of us, younger ones were together again, at Grandma Lamb's house.

You would have thought after everything we had been through with our stepmother, grandma would have been more sympathetic with us, but she was not.

Grandma did not know everything we had been through though not really, with our stepmother. She could only guess. We had been conditioned to not tell anyone anything. Even after Karen left, it got even worse for us.

Grandma saw enough to know it was not a very good situation for any of us. Grandma had quit visiting us because she was not allowed to visit with just her grandchildren. She had to spend time with our stepmother's children also. This made grandma mad. They were not even her step-grandchildren this was her son-in-laws wife, her daughter was dead, and she (our grandma) had been kicked out of the house where she had been living with us kids when the stepmother came along. The place where she had been raising us kids. Every once in a great while when it really got to grandma, not being able to see her grandchildren, she relented and had the stepmothers children as well as her grandchildren come to her house for a visit.

You would have thought that after we had not lived with her for so long she would have been different. She did not get to see us much, because the stepmother would not allow it. One would have thought that she would have been nicer. Nevertheless, grandma was still the same. In some ways, maybe even worse because she believed all the lies that the stepmother and grandma Baas was telling about us. How wild and out of control we were. Grandma Baas did not even know us. She did not even want to get to know us. If she did she did not show it.

Everyone knew the trouble John caused and he was the one example everyone used to judge the rest of us by.

Grandma worked the second shift. She worked at an old folk's home. She had been working there for many years. They all loved her. She was sixty-four years old now. She still had white hair, although it was a lot thinner than I remembered her hair to be. She still seemed old. She was tinier than I remembered or maybe I had grown a little taller. I looked down on grandma now. I was about four inches taller than grandma now.

It was a relief and a reprieve from all of grandma's shenanigans that she worked the second shift. This gave us all afternoon by ourselves. There was not an adult berating us at every turn. I was seventeen years old. I was old enough to watch everyone now and try to keep them out of trouble.

We did all of our own cooking now and even cooked for grandma. The stepmother had taught us this. We did all our own laundry and we did the cleaning. Grandma did not have to worry too much about getting things done. We knew how to help her do things.

Some of us made friends with the neighborhood kids. We stayed up late. There were not any kids my age to play with so I mostly stayed in the house, watching TV or listening to the radio. Practicing my dance moves. I still loved American Bandstand. It was a great way to learn how to dance.

There was one time in particular when the other kids took off to play and grandma went after them. I think she was afraid she would lose what temporary custody she had of us because she seemed more cautious than usual. She immediately jumped to all the wrong conclusions. She still thought the worst of all of us. We were good kids who got lost in the shuffle of bad parenting skills. Adults who did not know anything about kids or at least forgot what it was like to be a kid.

Yes! Perhaps they should not have gone and played with the neighborhood kids or gone behind the tracks so that grandma could not see them. She did not have to go off the deep end either. There just isn't any excuses for abuse.

I did not go out and play because I was seventeen. I felt I was too big to go outside and play. I did sometimes sit out on the porch and talk to the neighbors. I had been forced to give up a job, which I was pretty good at. It was hard to go back to being a kid when you cannot remember ever being one. You cannot go backward you can only go forward. I had not been allowed to go out and play like normal kids ever. I could not start now, not at seventeen.

Grandma had heard all the bad stories about how we would sneak out. Like all the adults in our life, she jumped to all the wrong conclusions.

No one ever thought to ask, "Why did you sneak out?" Everyone just assumed we did it because we were bad kids. That just is not true. Sure, on the surface it looks bad for kids to sneak outside to play. Remember we went from being allowed to play outside when grandma was with us, to a stepmother who locked us up at every turn. When we got a chance we wanted to play, so what choice did we have?

Truly I wish we would have been given a choice.

The stepmother did her very best to make us look bad at every turn. She did her best to say terrible things about us, to all who would listen.

Most people wanted to hear the worst and believe the worst, so they would not feel guilty.

After all the hard work grandma went through to get us to come and stay with her. I could not believe she was just as bad as she used to be.

We were so used to oppressive supervision, when we got freedom, people thought we were hellions, or so it seemed. We just liked to have fun and had very little knowledge of how we should do that. On the surface, it appeared as though we were hellions.

Grandma bought us some clothes. The stepmother never did get us our clothes. Therefore, grandma bought some clothes to get us through until we received our clothes from Harris Avenue. No one knew when that would be.

I was really surprised we did not get them right away. I shouldn't have been though. The stepmother never made it easy for anyone of us.

Chapter 5

Junior and Uncles take us to The Home

Have you ever felt scared about anything, I mean really scared! I was seventeen years old when I was placed in an orphanage, by the state authorities where I lived. My younger brothers and sisters were fifteen, fourteen, thirteen, and eleven. At first it sounded like an adventure. Once we got there it was anything but.

A few weeks after going to grandma Lamb's house, they (my oldest brother Junior, and one of my dad's brothers and one of my dad's brother's in law) Yes! Our uncles took us to the orphanage. We never did get our clothes or anything that belonged to us until we went to the orphanage. We never saw anything that our stepmother had packed for us until we got to the orphanage. We had no idea what was in our trunks.

We had to stop by Harris Avenue to pick up our trunks. They were not even delivered to us we had to pick them up. We were not allowed to get out of the old Ford station wagon, which took us to the orphanage. We could not go into our stepmother's house again. The house actually belonged to us. It was in our name. At least it used to be. Somehow she had finagled it so that she could keep both houses. She hired a shyster of a lawyer and she got to keep everything that was ours. We never stepped foot in either house ever again. We owned both houses 510 and 514 South Harris Avenue.

The stepmother gave each one of us trunk. All of our worldly possessions were in these trunks. All our clothes, shoes, hair accessories, books, toys everything the stepmother packed for us were in this one small trunk. The size was eighteen inches deep; three and a half feet long; by two feet wide with a big handle on it. The clothes she had packed were the worst of what we had owned. She gave us only what would fit into this one small little footlocker (trunk). If it did not fit into the footlocker, it now belonged to someone else the stepmother gave it away.

We took one of those old Ford station wagons with the three seats. The third one was facing backwards. All the trunks were on top fastened down to the top of the car. I was hoping the place I was going to, would be better than where I came from.

It was an hour's drive to get to the orphanage. Our oldest brother Junior and two of our uncles on our dad's side took us to the orphanage. The whole way there, they talked about how bad Grandma Lamb was. How she had killed her husband. How she was a drunk. We never knew any of this stuff. How it was because of her, her only son moved away from Ohio. It made me sick listening to the whole ordeal. How she was an alcoholic. How her husband was an alcoholic and a womanizer. On and on they went.

I felt they had no right to subject us to this kind of stuff. I was seventeen so it did not matter to me. I was thinking of the younger ones. I wanted to scream at them, to tell them they had no right to tell us these things. Debbie would be sixteen in a couple of months. Freddie was fourteen. Jimmy and Joan were both thirteen. Daryl was the youngest he was eleven. Daryl loved the ground that grandma walked on. She could do no wrong in his eyes. Grandma had raised Daryl since he was an infant.

Jr. said, "Do you know what your Grandma Lamb did to her husband? She killed her husband." "Didn't she kill her husband, Bob?" Yes that was just like Junior he didn't want anyone to know he was related to us. Junior said, "Your Grandma Lamb killed her husband" and it was his Grandma too he just didn't want anyone to know he was our older brother. It took me a long time to catch on but eventually I caught on. I don't blame him he was just ashamed of all the stuff that had gone on in our house. He didn't even call Bob an uncle and that is just what he was.

Uncle Bob said, "Yes that is exactly right."

Uncle Elton said, "Oh yeah! She killed him alright."

Not that any of these three people saw the killing they just heard things over the years and this is what they put together. None of it was true. We found out after we became adults ourselves that Grandpa Lamb had died when he was thirty five years old, he had syphilis or gonorrhea, but it was more dramatic to tell little children that their Grandmother had done such a heinous crime and killed her husband.

I was seventeen years old. The date was September 9th, nineteen hundred and sixty nine. We were on our way to an orphanage and this was the only thing my older brother could think of to say to us his younger brothers and sisters.

I was ten years old when he, Junior left our house on Harris Avenue and he was twenty years old.

No one else came along. I was just so dumb founded I was at a loss as to how to handle things, I cried silently. I did not make a sound for fear I would bring attention to myself. Instead of trying to reassure us that he would come to see us, he talked about how Grandma Lamb had killed her husband.

Grandma came in to help our Dad raise us after our Mother died, when no one else would. I was devastated and I had five younger brothers and sisters in the car with me. I did not want to hear about killing and dying. I wanted to hear they loved us and would come see us again. I felt like I was dying inside. I felt they were abandoning us. These people were supposed to love us. They were our family. Instead of them being upset that, we were going to an orphanage they were talking about killings and dying.

I felt like my guts were being ripped apart. I was scared. The elation and excitement of a new adventure had long since expired. I was the oldest of my dad's children living at home now. Except we no longer had a home. I was the oldest one of us six going to the orphanage. We were headed to our new home, a home like no other home we had ever been in before. An unknown, a place where we would know no one except each other, I wanted compassion and to be told that I was not being silly that things would be okay someday. I knew they would never be the same ever again.

I just did not understand why they could not talk of pleasant things like the weather! They could have reassured us that they would visit. They could have made sure we had their address so that we could write to them. They could have given us stamps and envelopes and stationary. They could have told us they would write to us. They did none of these things. They did not write us either. They just abandoned us. Some of us never saw our uncles again.

An hour after embarking on our journey, we arrived at our destination. Our brother and uncles left us there to fend for ourselves. The first place we went in the orphanage, after we checked in, was the hospital.

They did not make sure we were settled in okay.

They had done their duty. They discarded us into an orphanage. They could be done with us. They would not have to bother with us ever again and the uncles never did come and see us.

We never understood how our brothers, sisters, and uncles could just throw us away like this.

Junior is our brother and we saw him a little more often after we grew up. We did not see him much while we were in the Home. He had a family.

Once we arrived at the orphanage, the people in charge told us that we had been allotted five hundred dollars each to buy clothes. They said, "So where are the clothes that you were supposed to buy." We said, "We did not get any money for clothes."

They said, "Yeah! This is what usually happens. The money is not spent on the things for the students coming here." The people here were not the least bit surprised. The stepmother must have kept this money as well.

Now, I felt like even God had abandoned us. We were throw away children. We were unwanted children. Children no one loved. I know some of my brothers and sisters felt the same way. I should have asked God why? However, He was just another figure head (Father) that I couldn't trust. Back then I really didn't understand the complexities of a relationship with God. Also if God really existed how could He let this happen?

I was allowing Satan to cast doubts!

I have since learned that it was not God's fault. The adults in our lives made the choices.

Thank you God, for never giving up on me! Even though, it has taken me a long time to realize this.

The Front Gate

Chapter 6

Arrival at The Home

As we pulled up to the long driveway of the orphanage, the first thing that we saw, were these Civil War cannons. This did nothing to reassure me that we were somewhere safe. They were real live cannons. They were frightening and ominous looking, looming under, the bright sun. The sun seemed to make them look as if at any moment they could shoot at us instead of greet us. They looked at us just daring us to think we may have a safe haven here.

My brother and uncles were finally at a loss for words. I do not think they had ever come to check this place out, before we arrived. It was a bright sun-shining day in September of nineteen hundred and sixty nine when we arrived. They took us to the main building where someone was waiting to escort us to the hospital, where we would spend the next two weeks. Junior and my uncles could not go back to the hospital with us. I think they were just as happy not to have to go there with us. They never really had much to do with us before now.

We were at the orphanage. It was scary. The two big cannon ball guns standing at the entryway on top of cement walls. It seemed like this was a telltale sign of years long gone, protection from a war at some point in the history of the orphanage. The buildings were big and made of stone and brick and appeared to be over a hundred years old. They seemed dark and cold. They had just celebrated a centennial that year and there were some lingering signs still up from the celebration. This was another clue as to how old the buildings were and how long the orphanage had been in existence. The trees were all over grown and tall like they had been there awhile. It was a bright sun shiny day, it should have been cloudy and dreary, but it was not. I suppose I should have taken this as a sign from God that He would be there for us, no matter what.

After we were checked in at the administration building, we had to go immediately to the hospital. The next two weeks they ran a thorough battery of test. Every test imaginable was given to us.

They wanted to make sure we did not have any diseases or parasites to pass on to the other students in the orphanage. They wanted to verify the medical records we had brought with us. We had to have a complete physical before we came and another one when we got there. They wanted to make sure nothing was missed when they took custody of us.

The doctors and nurses gave us a complete physical. We were given many test; an oral test, a written aptitude test, plus a whole lot of other tests. It was unbelievable the amount of tests we had to go through. It seemed like weeks before we were finally allowed to leave the hospital and go to our cottages.

They stripped us down, or rather had us strip down. Then we had to put on hospital gowns. Just like at a real hospital. They wanted to check for deformities, abnormalities, and scars. Each one of us had several scars. Most of the scars were from falling down on our bicycles or from roller-skating or from climbing trees.

The Home had a full-scale, fully staffed hospital including, a dentist that came and checked our teeth.

They checked our weight and height and recorded this for our permanent records. We are checked for TB by giving us a TB test, which needed to be timed, this in itself took a few days to get the final results. We did not know this at the time that some of these test that we were given to us needed to be timed. They also wanted to make sure we were not carriers of any other kind of communicable diseases.

They had one nurse in particular whom everyone seemed to warn us. They said she was mean. She was the biggest woman I had ever seen. She was so large you could hear her coming long before you saw her and this was on concrete. She gave us the TB test. This test was not bad but the stories from the other students that she was mean, and big and scary were worse.

They checked our teeth for cavities; for crooked teeth; missing teeth, some of our teeth were pulled. They didn't bother trying to save them like they do today. Did not bother to try and fill all of them, just pulled them. Luckily, for us we didn't have crooked teeth, just a lot of cavities for lack of poor dental hygiene.

Taking care of teeth was not important to our parents or to our stepmother or our grandma. The stepmother still had all of her teeth but my dad had lost his teeth years ago; my mother when she was alive did not have her teeth; grandma did not have her teeth, so they all figured what was the use in taking care of your teeth when all you are going to do is loose them anyway. There wasn't a place to put such things as toothbrushes and tooth paste. There just was not enough space to put these things. On Harris Avenue we did not have enough space for all of us let alone for a place to hold something as mundane as a toothbrush.

We all did pass muster! Barely! Nevertheless, we must have passed all their tests.

We were eventually allowed to go to the main campus of the orphanage.

We never got a tour of the Home grounds. I thought this was pretty weird. Whenever you go to a new place everyone wants to give you a grand tour. People usually want to show off their place. We did not get one. This too should have been an omen to us that we would have to fight for the right to belong here, if we were going to stay here any length of time.

One of the other tests they did was, they checked to see if any of the girls were virgins. At the time, we did not understand this. Except maybe, they wanted to see how many of us were sexually active and could possibly be troublemakers. (Back then if you were sexually active you were a trouble maker.)

I fell out of a tree years ago and landed on a fence post. It pierced through me and it appeared as though I was not a virgin. They just assumed the worst. I did not realize what they were referring to when they made remarks like they did.

They (the adults) would say things, "Oh no wonder all the senior boys are getting dating passes." Or they would say, "We have some boys getting dating passes who have never gotten a dating pass before."

I was even allowed to go off the Home grounds in a car date, with one of the ex-pupils. I was a senior at this time although, I was not yet eighteen. He was over eighteen though. He took me to a movie, a drive-in movie. I found out later that he was surprised that I did not want to get into the back seat, to make out.

This is exactly what he had done with several of the younger girls. I was shocked and appalled. I was truly surprised that the adults of this facility thought this would be okay, for this overage ex-pupil to have sex or to go on a car date with a younger girl. They knew what was going on and did not try to stop it from going on. They not only allowed it to go on but encouraged it. They did not discourage this kind of behavior.

Contrary to what it looks like on the surface, we were not used to all this freedom. We did not know what to do with all this free time. I do not know if all of my brothers and sisters felt as I did. We never talked about it. We don't talk about our private feelings. We still to this day do not talk about it.

Where we came from, we were kept under a very tight leash. We were not allowed to go anywhere or be with friends our own age. We did not have friends to go anywhere with, even if we would have been allowed.

Where we came from no one wanted anything to do with us. They considered us white trash, even said as much. We looked trashy. We wore dirty, wrinkled clothes. We smelled of cigarette smoke. We had nasty looking teeth. Most of us looked unkempt. We needed a hair brush to brush our hair. Some of us smelled of urine.

There is that look that identifies your status in life and ours was this kind of status.

Administration Building

Chapter 7

Ohio Soldiers and Sailors Orphanage

By Jeff Denty

Information from: 'A Home of Their Own'

by Edward Lentz

Orange Frazer Press 2010

From its establishment in 1869 , until the doors were closed in 1997, the Ohio Soldiers and Sailors Orphans Home (OSSO) provided shelter for more than 13,500 children. At its peak there were over 900 children residing on the grounds known as Poverty Knoll, in southern Xenia Ohio.

The Home, as it was known to those who lived there, became a full service community for children who, for whatever reason, no longer had a place to call home. The working farm provided much of the food for the residents as well as valuable training for some.

There was also an on-site hospital, a chapel, and even a power plant for heating and electricity.

In the early nineteen seventies the population had dwindled to less than 400. These students were provided with a full education which included all the classes we would find in a public school, math, English, and science. It also included an extensive trade school.

The trades taught included, carpentry, baking, black smiting, barbering, and butchering. There was an active print shop, a shoe repair shop, a tin shop, and a laundry. There was a photography studio with a working dark room. Electrical and mechanical engineering were also taught. The goal was to teach skills that would provide a productive life for any young adult who had spent much time at all in The Home.

The Home Weekly, their own newspaper, was largely produced by the students. They learned the entire process, from finding and writing the stories to printing them. Stories included the most recent scores of The Cadets, their football team. What was playing at the local theater, and schedules for some of the on site facilities, such as the swimming pool. Anything that would be considered news for their small community was fair game.

The student's day was regulated by the blast of a steam whistle, as had been the case since the whistle was installed in 1873. The whistle indicated time to get up, time for meals, time for classes,

There were strict conduct and dress codes as one would expect from an institution set up by former military personnel for the children of military personnel.

In 1978, the name was changed to the Ohio Veterans Children's Home (OVCH) as they realized many of the children were not orphans in the traditional sense. Many still had one or both parents but for various reasons the parents were not able to provide for the children at that time.

In 1995 the Home closed its doors to incoming students and completely closed in 1997. The number of students had dropped considerably, and so had the financial and political support for the institution.

Hospital

Chapter 8

Virginal Girls

After several days of tests, the hospital released us. They said we would not contaminate any of the kids on campus. They did not say this in so many words but it was the message we received loud and clear.

At the beginning of the third week, we went to our respective homes or cottages as we called them. The first thing the younger girls were forced to do, was to strip naked.

The girls were ordered to try on all her clothes. Each and every single piece of clothing. Most young girls do not know how to say "No!" to anyone especially to an adult. We were no exception to this rule. At our house on Harris Avenue saying "No!" to an adult was grounds for a beating. The adults, excuse for making these girls try on their cloths, was so they knew what size they wore and to see if their clothes fit.

After the little girls took off all their clothes, they stood there naked trying to cover up with their hands. This did not work very well at hiding private areas. All four of these adults said in unison, "You do not have to cover yourself up from us. We are not looking at your body. We just want to make sure your clothes fit."

There were four adults watching. Four adults were ordering this exhibit. There were three female adults watching and there was one male adult watching these proceedings. I cannot believe no one ever stopped this interrogation. I still cannot believe that the adult women did not put a stop to it. At this tender age they are just beginning to have modesty. For this to be taken from them like this is devastating.

I just did not understand why these people had to do these things to these little girls. We had already been through a lot before we came here. Now to come here to this strange place with these strangers doing these things was horrible. What was the purpose! I did not understand what thrill they got out of it. What kind of perverts were they? To do something this degrading to little girls who were in an unfamiliar and scary situation already.

Was it their way of weeding out the submissive ones and the rebellious ones? Get rid of the rebellious ones because they would not conform to the rules, even if the rules were not in the best interest for the children involved? (Were they adult pervert child molesters in disguise?)

The little girls just cringed and tried not to submit. They could not say "No!" because we were taught to not ever say "No" to an adult. In the fifties and sixties, you were never allowed to say "No!" to an adult at least not in our house. On Harris Avenue if you said "No!" to an adult, it was another reason for a beating.

During the fifties and sixties the saying goes, "Children are to be seen and not heard." I guess this is one of those to be seen times.

The young ones just stood there, hung their heads, and took it all in meekly. It was from this day forward these girls decided they were going to run away. They wanted to get as far away as they could from this kind of treatment. Harris Avenue was bad. This kind of treatment was worse than our old life ever was. Harris Avenue they just beat you. Here they stripped you of what dignity you had left. By this time, we did not have any dignity or self-esteem left, it was already ripped away.

However, the worst was yet to come.

At night, all the young girls had to sleep naked in their beds. This was for what they called a panty check or a panty raid. That was when the Dean of the boys came into the cottage. He felt all the girls up one side and down the other. This is the worst of all treatment we ever received at Harris Avenue. The heartache we went through already to just come here for this is unspeakable hurt and harm and emotional damage.

If you got a spanking or a whipping, this male dean made you strip down and lay on his lap with your backside up. During the beating he took the time to feel and massage your backside yet again.

On Harris Avenue, we got plenty of beatings. The beatings were bad but went away after a while. We remembered them. Now to come here and be forced, to strip naked, and do these things was beyond our comprehension. This was low. If you had any dignity left it was gone now.

The cottage parent knew it and was there to watch and allow it to continue. Why did she allow it? What kind of a thrill did she get out of it? How could she force these girls into this kind of degradation and humiliation? What did this man give her in payment of her services and help to degrade these young girls?

Those girls who would not strip naked like the other girls went into solitary confinement. They had to conform to this new set of rules. She was not allowed to leave on her bra and panties. None of these girls knew how to say "No!" to these new adults in their life.

These were a new set of adults, a new set of rules being forced on us. The young girls had to do things they did not want to do. Each item seemed to be heavier and heavier; and harder and harder to put on.

How can any child survive such degradation? How can anyone survive this kind of treatment?

You would have thought that our previous experience with adults would have prepared us for this. I just did not know every adult was this bad. These adults set the bars so low it could not go anywhere but up from here or would it get worse.

When I heard about these things going on here I just could not believe it.

It made me want to throw-up I was so disgusted.

I never was an eyewitness to any of these proceedings but I was told of them on many occasions, by some of the other students. I was truly appalled when I heard of these proceedings going on at The Home.

I felt it was a misuse of power when these kids could not defend themselves. They needed a voice. They needed someone to protect them.

Peter Pan

Chapter 9

Me and Daryl

School had already been in session since, around the 1st day of September. So not only were we new kids we were late in arriving to the new school. The joke was on us. There was a nickname for new kids; they were called newkies so this became our nickname. We were the newkies.

After two weeks of being in the hospital, we went to our cottages. Daryl is the only one separated from us. He was not allowed to come and see us at all. We in turn were not allowed to see him. These were unspoken rules, which newkies did not know. Actually, we were all separated from each other. We were discouraged from seeing him and we were discouraged from visiting each other.

He was in the section called Peter Pan. This was for all the younger kids.

There was a junior campus for the middle graders as well.

There was one time I wanted to see my brother Daryl. They refused to let me see him. I threw a fit (today we would call it panic disorder or maybe post-traumatic stress disorder not as severe as the soldiers have). I started screaming at the top of my lungs and throwing a fit. All I wanted to do was to say, "Hi" to my littlest brother Daryl.

I had always taken care of these kids. After hearing what happened to the little girls, I felt they (the adults) must have been doing something wrong, to not let me see my little brother. After about thirty minutes of knocking on the door and no one even acknowledged that, I was even at the door. Someone finally came to the door. They told me if I would come back tomorrow, I could see him. This too seemed strange but I accepted it. What else could I do? I was not happy about it.

The next day, the same thing happened. I was really mad now.

If it was illegal, or against the rules, to visit with Daryl they should have told me, I did not know. I still would have wanted to see him. I started yelling and yelling and telling them if they did not let me see my brother and his room, I was going to call my caseworker. They did not want that, so they finally did let me in to see my little brother. I did that a lot this year. I am surprised they didn't lock me up. I would not have been able to handle that very well. They say God only gives you the things you can handle.

I think this was just my way of acting out. I had been through so many traumas already I just felt out of control here. I was not needed anymore. I was not wanted. Perhaps maybe I never was wanted. I was not alone in the feeling.

While I was visiting with him, he sat in the bottom of his locker. I said to him, "You can sit beside me on the bed."

He said, "No! I like sitting in the locker."

I said, "Are you sure?"

He said, "Yes! I am sure."

I thought this too was strange. He was grinning from ear to ear though so how was I to know any different. I could tell he was very glad to see me even if he had to sit in the locker while visiting with me. I did not know it at the time but he had been told to sit in the locker. It would be worse for him than it already was if he did not sit in this locker.

I did not want anyone to hear what I was saying to him. I was afraid he would get into trouble if people heard what I wanted to say to him.

He showed me his bunk, where he slept.

I just wanted peace of mind that he was ok.

Another way I was not conforming to the rules. I thought it a reasonable request to want to see my little brother. It had been well over two months since I had seen him. I was fuming. I did not want to have to call the caseworker. I did not know if I was capable of upholding that threat but I meant it. I would definitely have done just that. I wanted to make sure he was safe and to see if he was happy. He was really glad to see me, his big sister. There were rumors, of severe abuse going on in these little kids cottages as well. I wanted to see for myself that he was ok. He was sitting in a High School hall locker. It was not very big. I wanted to cry. He seemed like himself just different. I always took care of him.

I asked him, I said, "Are you happy?"

He said, "Yes!"

I said, "Do you like it here?" He said,

"Yes." I said, "Are you sure?"

He said, "Yes!"

If I had been more astute, I would have known this was his punishment because I had caused such a ruckus in wanting to see him. I should have known. We came from such abusive situations as it was. I did not think it could have been any worse than from where we came from. I could not have been further from the truth.

They slept in a large room on cots. He showed me his bunk, where he slept. I just wanted peace of mind that he was ok. It was pretty scary for me. I cannot imagine what it was like for the ones so young.

By focusing on someone else, I did not have to look at myself, to see how I was truly faring.

Again, I felt the urge to cry. If I would have cried, he might have cried too. I did not allow myself the self-indulgence.

I cannot imagine what it was like for him. Daryl was the youngest one of all of us who went to the Home. He too must have been scared. He did not show it. He just lit up like a Christmas tree. He was smiling from ear to ear. I knew it made him happy for me to be there. That whatever the punishment he got he knew it was worth it. His big sister loved him enough and cared about him enough to go and see him. If I had known all my brothers and sisters needed me I would have went to see them too. I did not know. They probably would not have talked to me anyway. By going to see Daryl, I was a non-conformist as it was.

There were about twenty beds in the one long sterile environment. I felt like it was my fault, we had all gone to the Home.

Grandma Lamb blamed me too! Because I told her what I had told the caseworker. I told her that I had told the caseworker, I felt she was too old. In reality, she did it to herself by telling the caseworker that boys will be boys. Every chance she got she blamed me; she told me it was my fault we had gone to the orphanage.

I felt really bad that Daryl was here all by himself here in Peter Pan, he never knew our mother. He always had his brothers, sisters, and Grandma

Lamb with him. Now no one whom he knew and loved was with him anymore; no one to protect him from the bullies.

Most of us went to the main campus so we did get to see each other almost every day. I did not see everyone though; I kept my eyes open for the possibility of seeing one of my brothers and sisters.

It was alien to me this new environment.

I am sure it was alien to Daryl and all of the rest of my brothers and sisters as well.

Hayes Hall (Senior Girls)

chapter 10

Senior Girls Day

Later in the year, the senior girls had a day they could invite any person they wanted to come and visit with them at their cottage.

Anyone at all, most girls invited their boyfriends. I did not invite my boyfriend. My boyfriend was very upset with me too. I invited my littlest brother Daryl, to come to my cottage. If I had known Freddie needed me, I would have tried to do something special for him too. If I had known Joan needed me, I would have tried to help her too. Daryl was the one we knew we were not allowed to visit with.

I knew Daryl did need me. I invited him to come over. When he came into the door, he was grinning from ear to ear. There was a hop to his step when he got excited about something. Yes! There was that little hop. He was excited to be here. I knew God had directed me to do this invite Daryl. I listened to the inner ear, which I now know was God talking to me. Daryl was happy to see me. My boyfriend was not.

My boyfriend said, "Why didn't you invite me to come over. You made me look bad with all the guys."

I said, "I did not know you needed to be invited. You can come over without an invitation whenever you like but my little brother cannot. I invited him to come. I knew you would come without an invite. You are here aren't you?"

My boyfriend said, "Yes! But you still should have invited me."

I said, "I knew you could come without an invite. You did not need a special invite. Seniors practically have free reign. I was only allowed one invitation."

I said, "Daryl needed to come and could not come without an invitation. You could come without an invitation."

I cared that he was upset. I could not undo, the invitation I had sent out, nor would I have. Daryl was happy, that was all that mattered to me. What was done was done. I was so used to taking care of my little brothers and sisters I needed to do this thing and invite my littlest brother to my cottage for the day.

The senior girls cooked for their guests. We played games all day long. We watched TV all day long. We could listen to music. The TV was set to the all-day John Wayne movies, which played every Sunday afternoon. We had a great time. They arrived shortly after lunch and left around seven pm. I think Daryl had a great time. One of the other girls in my cottage invited one of my other brothers so he also came for a visit.

Grandma Lamb had taught each one of us kids how to play euchre. We all loved to play euchre. We still do love to play euchre. It was one of those few fun things we were taught. Euchre was one of the few games we were allowed to play. She taught us open handed until we all learned how to play. It was fun. It was relaxing. It was crazy good fun. We took turns playing on two tables. Not everyone wanted to play. Those of us that did play euchre had a marvelous time. I was never so good that I would win every time. It was great to get a loner, though. A loner consisted of an Ace, King, Queen, Jack, or at least three, four, or five cards all in the same suit with a side ace. This was one time when the cards were stacked in your favor. If luck was on your side and you named trump, you knew you had a point; you got four points if you got all the tricks.

I was not the least bit intimidated that my boyfriend was upset with the arrangements I had made. It just made perfectly good sense to me. He could come over without an invite. My little brother could not. I wanted to make sure Daryl was still okay being here at the Home. I wanted to make sure no one was mistreating him. It probably did not make a difference whether I invited him or not. He probably would not have been able to tell me anything anyway. The code of silence we had learned on Harris Avenue still applied here. I did not ask anything except I wanted to make sure for myself that he was ok.

I am not saying I was a martyr. I was used to taking care of my younger brothers and sisters. It was a hard mold to break.

God gives you the insight to listen to your inner ear, when He is talking. It is up to you to listen to Him. This time I listened. I did not always make the wisest choices in my life.

We all had a good time playing cards and listening to music. We also watched John Wayne movies. Most people were John Wayne fans back then.

Daryl was from Peter Pan. It was not very often someone from Peter Pan, was invited to come up to the main campus. Daryl was excited about coming. All of Daryl's friends were envious that he was allowed to come up to the senior girl's cottage, he told me so.

We ate supper. We had popcorn as a snack later on. It was a lot of fun. I had two of my brothers in my cottage. It was really nice that one of the other senior girls had invited one of my other brothers too.

We were only allowed one visiting guest per person and mine was Daryl. My boyfriend was also a senior. Senior boyfriends were allowed to come and go. So this was not the normal situation having two guests.

Daryl was happy. He looked happy. He was having a good time playing cards. This is really all that mattered to me.

Jimmy too had fun! He had made friends with a lot of the senior girls.

Norma Jean at Hayes Hall

Chapter 11

Me (Norma Jean) at The Home

Now it is my turn, I get to the senior cottage and all the rooms are full. No one wants the newkie in their room. They did not want me invading their space and territory. I do not blame them. For me it was just another form of the rejection I had been receiving all my life. I was used to it by now or pretended to be. It did not make me feel any better.

It was the fourth week of school. You think you are going to have a room to yourself as a senior. All of a sudden, you have to share your room. I was not wanted. I would not have wanted to share my space with a perfect stranger either. Who knows what kind of a person this new girl was going to be. I am sure they were thinking I might steal their stuff. Take something that does not belong to me.

I think that is why I tried so hard to make sure all the rest of my brothers and sisters had a better time coping.

The adults did not know what to do with me at the Home. It was rare if ever that a senior came to the home. I really had no place else to go. My parents were dead. Grandma Lamb did not want me without my siblings. Grandma Baas definitely did not want me. I was too old for everyone. They felt I would be too defiant to come and stay with anyone. The authorities said I could stay with my stepmother. That would not have helped me any. I did not feel that was in the equation. I hated that place. I hated Harris Avenue.

After hanging out in the living room for about two weeks the cottage house parent told the girls they had to make space for me. I would take my shower and brush my teeth in the bathroom. I dressed in the bathroom. The houseparent said, "It would be the girl's decision to decide who would take me into their room but they needed to let me have some space."

I finally got a space. I just had one trunk with all my worldly possessions in it. I just needed a bed. I did not have enough clothes to need a closet.

I felt I was not coping very well and I wasn't.

One day I took a shower and while I was in the shower, I just started shaking all over and crying. I was afraid someone was going to come in and give me a beating, for taking a shower in the middle of the day. I broke out into a cold sweat when I was done. It was like I was in a trance, being teleported back to Harris Avenue, about to get a beating. It was scary.

The senior girls ate most of their meals in their cottage except lunch. This was to teach us how to cook. This was to teach us portion size. When we graduated, these skills would help us to manage our own place.

My cottage parent was really, nice. She taught me that it is ok to look out for myself for a change. She said, "It is just too bad that you had so much responsibility for one so young and for so many years." She also said, "It is too bad you did not have time to do homework. You could start now and learn how to do homework." No one had ever cared enough about me to tell me to do my homework. No one ever gave me the time to do homework. It was sad too, to think that I am a senior and did not know how to do homework.

I was great on the home front. I could cook, clean, and babysit like the best of them. I knew very little about actual schoolwork. I did not have any social skills. How I got this far is beyond me. I did not know how to take care of me. I did not know this was even something I was supposed to do. I always took care of others.

I had a few great teachers along the way that took a special interest in me and gave me extra attention. But mostly they could only help before and after school. It was never allowed.

My cottage parent said, "It was a shame you did not learn how to take care of yourself."

For so many years, I had to look after so many kids.

She said, "It was sad that for so many years you had the responsibility of watching all my younger brothers and sisters. She said, "You were too young for such a big job."

I had never thought about it before but she was right. She said she would teach me this aspect of life. She made it her mission to teach me that it was ok to take care of me.

So this was my first lesson, it was ok for me to do homework. I already knew how to cook. She taught me how to teach the other girls how to cook. She had me teach them how to make a menu. She had me teach them how to make a grocery list from that menu. It was neat. I felt like I was useful again.

It was still sad too because I loved my brothers and sisters. They did not seem to need me anymore. After about a month, we seemed to be settling in nicely.

They taught me how to sew.

I learned how to type, which is still useful today.

I learned to take shorthand, do not remember any of it now though but it was interesting.

It was devastating in the beginning but I did learn to cope.

It was good for me to learn the skill of taking care of me. After all, my brothers and sisters would not graduate with me. I would not be able to take them with me. They were wards of the state now. They were out of my jurisdiction.

One other thing the kids in the orphanage did for the newkie.

They wanted to play a prank on me the new senior girl.

They nominated me for homecoming Queen. I was excited. I was honored. Nothing like this had ever happened to me before.

The joke was on me. They started insinuating how much she meaning me, did not deserve to be Queen. I did not deserve to have this honor. This honor was meant for home kids only. Not an outsider I was still an outsider. I had not been there long enough. Yes! It was meant for someone who had been there a while, not a newkie. I heard many of the kids say this. I don't think they meant for me to hear this but I did. One would think maybe they did mean for me to hear this?

At least I was in her court. I was in the Queen's court. I was runner up. The girl they nominated was beautiful. She had been there nine years. Yes! She deserved it. She was sweet natured and had a kind heart.

After the nomination, I just felt bad. The pleasure I had felt at just being nominated was taken from me. I was still thrilled though just not as thrilled. I was glad and happy for the girl who was nominated because she had always been nice to me.

The Queen went out on the dance floor first with her partner. Then her court went out to dance with her and their partners. It was fun. In the public school, I had never been nominated for anything, and would not have been permitted to go even if I were nominated. Therefore, I was not going to allow the rumors and gossip to ruin this for me. I had never had a date to a dance before. I was not trying to be selfish or anything I just wanted to have fun. I had never been to a school dance before.

There was still that niggling little doubt that perhaps I did not belong.

It was homecoming.

To this day since I was only in the Home for my senior year some of the kids, (now adults) think I have no right to claim the orphanage as my home. I know because they have told me this to my face.

Chapter 12

Debbie At The Home

Everyone gets to the point where you have just had enough. Unfortunately, for Debbie the time was now. She just could not take any more abuse from the adults in her life. At this point, she had lost both of her parents. Our mother died when she was five years old. Our dad died when she was fourteen. She had both of her grandmothers but neither one of them wanted her. Heck, they did not want any of us for that matter. If our grandparents had wanted any of us than we would not be here in this place we would be with them.

She felt like an unloved, unlovable child.

As I told you in the beginning Debbie was tiny. Most of the girls in the Home were bigger than Debbie. This put Debbie at a disadvantage, being the tiniest in your class.

It seemed to bother some of us more than others that no one wanted us. We called ourselves the unloved unlovable throwaway kids.

She had taken about as much as she could take.

Debbie got into an argument with her cottage supervisor (houseparent). This woman was trying to take away Debbie's trunk. This was the only thing she had left of Harris Avenue. We did not have parents. This is all that was left of our parents, our memories, and Harris Avenue. Not very many of your possessions would fit into something so small. We did not have too many possessions but do not take what few possessions we have away from us. The trunk was a three feet long by two feet wide. It was a symbol. This was a symbol of a lost and broken childhood.

If you could put a parent's love into this trunk, this would be what it represented. It was representative of everything she had lost. It represented all the abuse she suffered so far.

I can understand where Debbie was coming from. She did not want to lose the last vestige of her identity. Taking this trunk away would do that to her.

My houseparent came and told me. They had put Debbie into isolation. I was shocked. Our stepmother used to keep us locked in the basement. None of us dealt well with being locked in a room. It made most of us claustrophobic.

I was furious. I told them that other students had done worse and nothing happened to them. I told them (the people in charge that is) that some of the students had fistfights with their teachers and nothing happened to the students. A fistfight between an adult and a student seemed much worse to me (I said as much). Yet nothing happened to these students. I said, "Debbie just argues with a houseparent and you lock her away." I just did not understand why the double standard. Why make an example of Debbie? They just laughed in my face. I was infuriated.

I told them I wanted her out or we could go to court. By this time in my life, I did not care either what they did to me. I had been through too much already myself, to let them do this to one of my brothers and sisters. They could throw me out of the orphanage, then what. Who would care? I certainly did not care.

I learned much, much later on that another reason they put her into solitary confinement was that she refused to go to bed without her under panties. The Dean of boys could come in and feel them up at night. She refused to allow it. Debbie still had her panties on, so she was not as easily accessible as the other girls were. The house parent would come in and do a panty check (for easy access for the dean of boys), she would make Debbie take off her under panties and as soon as the house parent left she (Debbie) put them back on.

After everything else we had already been through, I thought this was really bad. I thought it was disgusting for a grown man and for a house parent to do this. She just seemed to have one problem after another. Debbie refused to conform. If this was the only thing she would not conform to than I am proud of her for not conforming. She was not going to have them make her do something she knew was not right.

This house parent controlled everything. What under panties to wear. What clothes to wear and when to wear them.

There was another time Debbie locked herself in her bedroom. She did not let the houseparent into the room. All the girls were cheering her on. This helped her to be a big person on campus. The older girls however picked on her ferociously. Debbie did take a stand for herself and I am glad she did. She needed to before she lost herself forever.

It is about time too.

When you are under oppression, you can only take so much. Debbie was finally sticking up for herself. The Dean of boys really liked Debbie. He never got a chance to feel her because she would not go without her under panties at night.

This person had her put into solitary confinement.

This was not the only time they put Debbie into isolation. They put her there also when her houseparent accused her of bleeding (having her monthly cycle) and not cleaning up her mess. She said, "I am not on my period."

The houseparent said, "You are too and these pads and underwear are yours. You left the sheets in the bathroom too."

After several times of arguing back and forth and back and forth between Debbie and her cottage parent, the underwear in question was in fact not Debbie's but someone else's.

I thought it was quite ingenious for her to come with an idea on how to solve it.

Debbie said, "I did not leave that mess behind. It is not my mess. We can solve this problem though. We will check everyone's mattress." They checked every mattress. There was no blood on any of the mattresses. Then Debbie said, "Let's flip the mattresses over." They proceeded to flip all the mattresses over and sure enough, there was not any blood on Debbie's mattress. There was blood on one of the other girl's mattresses.

The one time that I found out Debbie was in isolation I told them to get her out and get her out now. If they did not I would go to the authorities and tell them the problems we were having here. They did get her out.

She did manage to get a couple of house parents to take her under their wing. She did not make friends easy; most of the kids thought she was trouble. They picked on her at every turn. Just because she was finally sticking up for herself, they picked on her.

These kids did not know what we went through before we got there. They just thought most of us were troublemakers.

This cottage house parent decided to not deal with the big girls anymore and moved to Peter Pan.

The Farm

Chapter 13

Freddie in the Home

Freddie was different. He was tall, lean and lanky. His feet grew faster than he did. So his big feet were always in the way making him appear clumsy. That old adage that he had to grow into his feet Yep! That was Freddie. He was so gullible. People would take advantage of this. The boys were the worst culprits.

They ganged up on Freddie on more than one occasion. A group of four or five guy's at a time were involved at least twice, that I know. They did everything imaginable to him. Boys can be very abusive, to the boy who appears different or weak. Freddie never squealed. Everyone knows what happens to squealers, it just gets worse. The bullies became even more aggressive and more abusive.

Freddie didn't really talk much about it to us. Just mentioned it in passing a time or two or when he got mad and was chewing God out for something he would mention it. He did that a lot, got mad at God, for allowing all this ugliness to happen to us. He did what the rest of us were afraid to do. Yell at God. We wanted to but we never did. The rest of us were afraid to berate God.

Jimmy tried to defend Freddie as often as he could but that only made it worse. When Jimmy's back was turned and they got Freddie alone the boys did even more damage to Freddie and picked on him more than they otherwise would have done. Jimmy could not protect Freddie in this environment twenty-four hours a day seven days a week. The boys waited and bided their time until he was alone.

He had been so different from our other brothers. Even our own brothers used to pick on him. Our dad would then laugh about it later. The teachers used to pick on the weaker ones too. There just was not any hope for the weaker ones. It was a winner take all kind of a place. Everywhere we went; it was a winner takes all kind of a place. None of us ever caught a break.

Freddie said he used to cry every night when he was in the orphanage. Especially on those rare occasions when his older brothers and sisters would come back for a visit and leave him there all alone, Jimmy, Joan and Daryl were still there but Freddie hated the orphanage, with a passion and everything it stood for. Not that we had it better where we came from it was just another place to abuse us. Freddie had us there, he doesn't have us here.

When we become adults and our youngest brother died, I had trouble leaving the funeral home. I said out loud to no one in particular, "I hate to leave him alone we have been left alone so many times." I know it sounds crazy, he is dead, he is not here, but his body the way we knew him was here. I just had trouble leaving. When I said it out loud, Freddie came up behind me and said, "Me too." Both of us were crying. It was a crazy thing to say, he's dead. I think Freddie was also thinking of all those times in the orphanage when his older brothers and sisters left him behind to fend for himself. It made us both cry all the more.

He did not make friends very easy. Actually very few of us did.

Jimmy did make friends easy. He just did not understand how the rest of us could not make friends.

Freddie did come to terms with his time at the orphanage. He had nowhere else to go.

Freddie learned some good skills here at the orphanage too, so it wasn't all bad. The first thing he learned was farming. The orphanage had its own farm. Here we had milk cows. They provided all our milk. It was the best milk we had ever had. It was ice cold and fresh from the cows. It doesn't get any better than that.

The people who worked the farm had to get up early to milk the cows so that the milk was on the table and ready for breakfast.

There was a time when the Home grew all of the food that was eaten by the orphans and the staff. Over the years this dwindled down to where we produced less and less of our own food.

They used to have beef cattle, and pigs. They used to do all their own butchering. Quite an undertaking, this is the part Freddie exceled at, he was good with the animals and good with the farm equipment. Farming was not as high in demand as it once was.

Still, Freddie loved it.

The other thing Freddie was good at, he was good at printing. This was another skill he learned, an old-fashioned printing press. Being a printing press operator is a skill that has gone by the wayside today, with modern technology. In its heyday, the printing press was a very desirable skill to have

Freddie was really good at typesetting the printing press.

Most of his jobs as an adult, he was a printer in some form or other. Now with the modern age he is not in high demand.

Freddie even started his own business for printing when he became an adult.

Freddie also took up horticulture. He loved the study of plants. He loved to watch them grow and figure out how to make them grow better. He also wanted to know what they were beneficial for.

Don't get me wrong Freddie was not an angel.

He had a temper and anger issues.

We all had anger issues. We still have anger issues at times. It is how we deal with these issues that get us into trouble.

The Trades Building

Chapter 14

Jimmy at the Home

Jimmy is a twin. He is Joan's twin brother.

Jimmy had dark brown hair and dark brown eyes. Both of these features he inherited from our mother. He had a ready smile.

He seemed to do the best at the Home. He was the type that does not know a stranger. He never did know a stranger. He always made friends with ease. Out of all of us God gave him the talent to gab. He made lasting friends.

One of his best friends married his twin sister. He did not come out unscathed, though. He is a workaholic.

Jimmy is very outgoing. He makes friends easy, unlike the rest of us. Everyone seems to gravitate towards Jimmy. Everyone loves his friendly outgoing, enterprising personality. The rest of us were quiet and shy. We did not make friends easy.

Jimmy's enterprising ways earned him a reputation to getting things done. He had a paper route before we went to the Home. His customers loved him; he always received lots of tips.

We did not know how to converse with others. Some of us still have this trouble. We do not know how to keep a conversation going. We can ask people questions but to communicate back and forth on a give and take basis, it is not there. We were and still are to some degree backward. This made some of us a target for bullying.

Jimmy tried to protect those of us who were less aggressive. Those who did not make friends as easy but he could not be there twenty-four seven. The more Jimmy tried to protect the more the bully's went out of their way to cause trouble.

Everybody liked Jimmy. The teachers liked Him. All the other kids like him. All the adults in charge liked him. He was and still is an enterprising person. He saw something he liked he went after it.

It seemed like nothing bothered Jim. He was going to make the best of every situation. He just treated the Home as if it was just another place to live for a while. He had to be there until he was old enough to go out on his own. He did not seem to mind. He was not going to let it get him down. If someone said, anything negative he tried to give positive feedback instead. If he was ever down he was not down for long. His whole outlook on life in general was and still is positive. If you thought negative thoughts, he tried to give positive thoughts to replace them.

For this entire positive attitude, everyone liked him.

He like his twin sister earned extra privileges too, at the Home. When you earn extra privileges, you get to do a few extra things to help some of the adults. He did not cause trouble. Most of the people who picked on the underlings left Jimmy alone. Jimmy used words instead of fists to fight his fights.

The Home had its fair share of bullies, just like anywhere else. If you didn't fit into the mold you were picked on. No one likes to be picked on. Jimmy tried to protect not only his brothers and sisters from the bully's, but other kids in the Home who were always being picked on as well.

The Home was good for Jimmy he made friends here, the kind that lasts a lifetime.

He was that all around good American boy.

He was good with sports. Jimmy was on the football team. He was on the basketball team. He was on the track team. He was on the baseball team. He was also on the drill team. He did all these things really well too. Everything he did he excelled with ease.

He got really good grades. He was nominated to go to Boy's State, which is an honor for high achieving students. He was chosen as an alternate though. He hated being second place. He hated being last most of all.

He applied himself. He earned a good reputation. He got things done, when he started things, he finished them.

He was the first one of us kids to go to college after High School.

The Home was a military home and school. The boys were expected to be in R.O.T.C. The rankings were as in any other programs of R.O.T.C. There were the officers. Jimmy was an officer. He did everything with precision. This is something else where he excelled. He was good at commanding people's attention. He was good at the precision fine-tuning of the people under him. The Home had an excellent R.O.T.C. program.

Jimmy didn't like negativity. He wanted to forget his past. He wanted to pretend it did not exist. Well maybe not pretend it did not exist he just didn't want to be bothered with remembering it. He thought remembering it did not do any good. He did not want to dwell on the past. He wanted to make a living, and become rich and famous. Rags to riches, is what he always called it. Remembering his past was not going to make this happen. Remembering the past did not make him happy. It was depressing. By dwelling on it and remembering it put us right back there and he was never going back to Harris Avenue again.

He thought if he worked hard and kept his nose, clean things would fall into place.

Even as an adult, when we got together as a family, he did not want to talk about the past. He preferred to leave the past in the past, where it belongs. He felt the past was the past.

He does talk about it now with his friends. He does not want much to do with the family. When he sees us, it reminds him too much of the past and he cannot stand, what he sees.

As in everything else, his positive outgoing personality does not lead to his family ties. He keeps his distance so that he can remember only those positive thoughts that have kept him going all these years.

as the colonel, he was in charge of the whole

The Photo Lab

Chapter 15

Joan at the Home

Joan was Jimmy's twin sister. She was the younger of the twins. Jimmy was born five minutes before Joan.

Joan was the exact opposite of Jimmy. She had blue eyes and light brown hair that turned darker as she aged.

Joan was quiet and shy. She was endearing everyone liked Joan.

Joan got the brunt of the male teasing when we first got to the Home, probably because she was the youngest of us girls. She was very cute and very tiny and petite.

They would chant, "Hey Bass tell your sister I want some ass. (Baas which is normally pronounced B-ah-ah-s, they pronounced it bass to rhyme with ass)." On and on they would go. It was very degrading for her. It was degrading for any of us who happened to hear it as well. None of the adults would stop them from using this vulgar, kind of slang. No one ever stopped the kids from using the vulgar connotation our whole life. It was just acceptable.

Then one day, the barbs and teasing got so bad, one of the students even kicked Joan in the chest and stomach area. This boy was tired of Joan ignoring him, so he kicked her. He kicked her so hard and with all his might that she doubled over in pain and fell to the ground. He had knocked the wind completely out of her. It was a long time before she could catch her breath; it was an even longer time before she could get herself off the ground, from where she had fallen, she was hurting so bad. She had a huge imprint on this area too, where he had kicked her. She also had huge bruise that lasted several weeks.

Joan was only four foot nine inches and weighed only eighty-five pounds, when she was full grown. She was really tiny. The guy who kicked her was almost six feet tall and had to have weighed around one hundred and sixty five pounds or a hundred and seventy pounds. The size difference alone was enough to make the kick be pretty hard.

He tried to apologize later, because he felt bad, but the damage was done. It was hard for Joan to forget and forgive, being kicked in the chest. It was ridiculous. He did this just because Joan was ignoring him and his buddies and their rude chanting comments.

They did virginity tests on all the new girls. They found out that Joan's older sister (me), was not a virgin. Not in the typical sense, I was not a virgin! I fell out of a tree when I was younger, landed on a fence post, and lost my virginity. They thought I would be easy prey. Even some of the adults thought I would be easy prey. There were never any doctors called to our house nor did I go to a Doctor's office. There were no records of me, falling out of a tree. They never verified the damage done. Just a young girl without anything to prove she was still a virgin. No records to prove she was still innocent. Just adults insinuations that the evidence that was inside her body did not lie, that she was still a virgin.

It was just adults spreading rumors. It was boys being interested in an easy lay or an easy target.

Rumor was, Joan's older sister would put out because she was not a virgin. All they had to do was ask me if there was ever a time that I had sex. I could have told them flat out "No!" I would not have known that I lost my virginity. I did not know what that was. I fell out of a tree. I landed on a fence post. I started bleeding very badly and it hurt really, bad. I never went to see the Doctor. It cost too much money. The kids and the adults probably would not have believed me anyway. It would have been a bigger joke to them.

Joan was ready to run away. She hated the place in the beginning. It was, for her, worse than a nightmare.

This was the only thing worse was Harris Avenue and living with our stepmother. A couple of other boys from my class stopped her from running away for which I have always been grateful to them. It is hard to tell what would have happened, if she had run away.

Finally, the science teacher made a comment, to give her a challenge that forced her to care; about life again. He said, "Are you going to just quit? Just give up? You could prove them all wrong and fight. You can fight for yourself for a change."

This challenged Joan, as she had never been challenged before. Until now we were never allowed enough time to do homework. At least some of us, were not allowed this precious time. Some of us were always too busy taking care of others and doing manual labor around the house to have time for things like homework. Joan decided she was not going to give up. She was not going to let them win. She was going to prove them all wrong. She was going to make sure they ate their words. She was going to fight for the right to care again. She was going to fight for the right to be a good student; fight for the right to fight for herself for a change.

The first week Joan was in her cottage here at the home, her house parent made her sit by herself at the lunch table. Her cottage was assigned two tables. Each table in the mess hall was round and large enough to fit around twelve chairs comfortably. All the other girls, in Joan's cottage and the house parent sat at one table. Joan sat by herself at an entirely different table. Like, she was an outcast. Joan's house parent was punishing her just because she was a new student. It was very humiliating. Everyone stared at her, like she had done something wrong. She had done nothing wrong. She was new, a new kid in the class. We have all been a new kid or new adult at some point in our lives so we know how this feels.

I felt so bad for her. I asked my house parent if she could sit with us. I was afraid this would get her into more trouble. My house parent (Mrs. Henson) said, "I see no reason why not." I walked over to Joan who was sitting clear on the other side of the room and asked her if she would like to sit with us at the senior table.

Joan was shaking uncontrollably. She was crying, tears were streaming down her face.

(That took guts on my part. Just another way I thwarted authority) Joan's houseparent did not approve but she did not stop it either. She gave me a dirty look when I went to get my sister but she did not say anything. She had that look that said I will kill you for this. I didn't care. I missed a step walking but I didn't care.

It was special to sit at the senior girl's table with your older sister. I guess this proved I was not a conformer either. I just could not stand it a moment longer. The only time the senior girls ate in the cafeteria was for lunch. For the other two meals, I do not know what went on, probably, the same kind of punishment of Joan sitting by herself.

The next time I saw Joan sitting by herself, I asked Joan again, "Would you like to sit with me at my table." Joan said meekly with tears in her eyes, "ok." It was a shame, to leave anyone sitting all alone, in a big hall to eat by herself. Joan just started crying and shaking she was so distraught over the situation. I felt really bad for my sister. This was her punishment for being the new kid on the block. How can any adult treat a child this way? If you hate your job that much get out.

God Bless Mrs. Henson. She allowed me to go and get my little sister. Joan ate lunch with us. This went on for at least a week.

As I walked the full length of this dining hall, I felt all eyes were on me. My face turned red, I felt hot all over, like I was doing something wrong. I almost panicked and went back to my seat but God wanted me to protect my brothers and sisters and stand up for them. I was not going to stop now. I had gotten beatings before. I did not know if I would have gotten a beating for this offense. I did it. I walked proud. I knew God planted the seed. He wanted me to take full charge. I did have permission didn't I? From my house parent. Yes! I did have permission.

I was planning to have her eat with us at the senior table every day until she could sit with the other kids in her cottage. I think she did a couple more times too, sit at our table and eat with us. I suppose Mrs. Henson was not a conformer either. I think Mrs. Henson had a soft spot for our whole family. Joan's houseparent did not. She did not like me going and getting Joan to have her eat at the senior table.

It was bad enough when kids treat other kids this way but for the adults to be this way is a shame. From that day forward at lunchtime, when Joan was sitting by herself, I went and got her to sit at the senior. After about a week, her cottage parent relented and let her eat at their table, with her and the other girls.

It was one thing for me to be defiant at our home on Harris Avenue quite another to have such a captive audience for something so bold. Defying the laws of this new place, it was bold and audacious of me.

She did finally do ok at the orphanage and even made a few lasting friends. As a senior, she went to girls' state, which was a great honor. To be able to go to girl's state you had to be the best of the best. You had to be nominated by your teachers. Joan became an honor's student.

Joan eventually got special privileges. She got to work on the switchboard at the Home. This was a paid position. She loved this job.

She also was one of the lucky ones who earned the privilege of helping to serve luncheons at special board meetings and banquets. She received tips too for this privilege, which she was allowed to keep for herself as spending money.

She eventually learned to help the cooks. When a special event came up, they taught her how to set up the tables. She also learned how to waitress the tables.

She also joined the photo club. In this club, she learned to take pictures and to develop film in a dark room. She learned just how to position the subjects, so they turned out even better. I think she loved the photo club and photo lab best of all the things she did in the Home.

Joan took cosmetology. She did a learned a lot about dress designing too.

She met her husband here at the Home. She made several good friends here too. She did well.

Daryl and his bike

Chapter 16

Daryl at The Home

Daryl was our youngest brother. Every one of us tried to protect him. When we went to the orphanage, we were separated from each other. We could no longer help each other. Some of us felt this was a hindrance. We had always had each other to rely on. Now we had to rely on ourselves.

It was probably God's design for us to rely on someone else other than siblings.

The first category that separated us was age. The little ones had a campus all their own. Then they had the middle campus for the in between age and then there was the campus for the older kids.

The next category that separated us was sex. The females had their own cottages and the males had their own cottages, this was all done according to age as well. The younger kids were also separated by grade levels as well.

There were two sides to the Home. There was the boy's side and the girl's side. The Main Building and the Mess Hall, which was connected to the main building is what separated the girl's side from the boy's side. There was also an armory, which was behind the Main building and mess hall.

Daryl had been picked on so much by our stepmother and her older children, we all worried about him. I was not the only one to worry about him. (In our family as one would age we started taking care of the younger children in the household.) We did not know how he would fair here. He was a quiet boy. He never complained about anything. You hardly knew he was around.

There was not any way we could protect him anymore. We did not even get to see him every day. They would not let us visit back and forth with each other let alone visit with the little kids. They went to units or cottages all by themselves with a campus all their own. We were not supposed to visit them under any circumstances.

Family units did not exist here. Our family became the kids in our cottages. Oh everyone knew who had the same last name and who was related to whom. But from this time on the family unit as we knew did not exist.

This scared me a lot. I was not allowed to see my other brothers and sisters either. I could see them at the mess/chow hall or on the way to school. It was not privately or for very long. About all you had, time to do was say hello. There were times though that if one was brave enough or inventive enough you could sneak away and go visit.

Sometimes I would catch a glimpse of Daryl when he was on his way to school. He had to walk right passed the senior girls cottage. I would shout out his name. He would start grinning from ear to ear and there would be a little skip in his step, like to say I had just made his day. His classmates all liked it too. They would say things like, "There she is! There's your big sister." They would be smiling and waving too. I tried to see him every single day. I made sure I said, "Hello!" to Daryl before I would leave for school. I would have walked with him to school too if I would have been allowed. I was not allowed. Daryl and his classmates and he had to walk single file all the way to school. They lived and walked a good distance away to get to the school, not very far really. Not like what we had to do in the public school system where we came from. Just farther than most of us students. I suppose that was to make sure we were still kept separated from the younger ones.

I was advised, it was against the rules and regulations for me to walk Daryl to school. I really wanted to though. I just wanted to visit with him and talk with him. School was not that far from the senior girl's cottage. What kind of trouble could I cause just walking with him across the street?

Daryl was in the Home the longest out of all of us.

As Daryl aged, he started having nervous disorders. He used yoga as a relaxation method. He did it faithfully his nerves were so shot from everything he had been through thus far.

Then one day one of his teachers told him, "Take this pill and you won't need the yoga ever again." He took the pill. He never used yoga as a relaxation method again.

Daryl was hooked on pills, then alcohol, then the combination of all of it.

This first pill was the first of many years of drugs and alcohol abuse for Daryl, because an adults took it upon themselves to steer him into a life of drugs and alcohol. Sure, the drug of choice for this teacher may have been harmless but to a sensitive kid who knew nothing but abuse from adults it was devastating. He was never the same after this. He would sneak into the alcohol also when he came for a visit.

I just cannot believe any adult (teacher) would do something so horrific as to encourage (teach) a student to use drugs as an alternative to yoga.

Daryl spent several more years in the Home after we all left. We all tried to get him out for vacations and things occasionally. Some of us even tried to adopt him or at least get him out permanently but he did not want to leave. He eventually learned to like it there. He made many lasting friends.

One of the skills Daryl learned here at The Home was woodworking. He was very talented. Quite a few of us still have some of the pieces of furniture he made. He made grandma Lamb a china hutch. She put her set of Friendly village dishes on this hutch. This was grandma's pride and joy. Partly because it was made by her pride and joy (Daryl) and it was a really nice piece of furniture. Some of the rest of us have other pieces of furniture he made, like stools and shelves.

The Back Gate

Chapter 17

Dating Pass

In order for any of us students to date another student here at the Home, we had to ask for permission and apply for a dating pass. Most of the time there was not a problem in getting a dating pass. If you were a student who seemed to always cause trouble or were on detention for an offense, or suspension you did not get a dating pass. This did not happen very often. Most of us wanted to stay out of trouble so that we could get a dating pass. We were allowed extra privileges if we stayed out of trouble.

One of the things we were allowed to do with a dating pass was go to the movies. We had our very own private movie theater here on the Home grounds. They played a lot of good movies here. We were allowed to hold hands with our boyfriend or girlfriend and walk down to the theater where the movies were being shown. You had to have a dating pass in order to have this privilege of walking with your boyfriend or girlfriend to the movie house. The adults knew who the students were; who were always in trouble and probably did not have a dating pass. They did not even need to ask most of us, to see our dating pass.

We sometimes were allowed to walk downtown, to downtown Xenia, Ohio. We needed a pass for this as well. We sometimes had to show our passes to the stores where we shopped. I never had this happen to me, but I did hear of others who had to show their passes. This was our proof that we had permission to be downtown. The day we would go down to town we had to ask for permission of our house parent before we could go and usually we were given a time limit as to when we were expected to be back. We were never allowed past the dinner whistle. My favorite place was Woolworth's Department store. They had a great soda fountain there. We could get hamburgers, french fries and a soda fountain drink. They had great penny a candy section.

Woolworth's was an all-around great store. It also had clothes that were not too expensive.

It was fun especially to a kid that had never been allowed to do anything remotely like this before. I was never allowed to go to the store for just window-shopping before, or for daydreaming. It was quite a unique experience. Having this much freedom to me was mind-boggling. To experience little everyday things that kids take for granted. It was totally foreign and mind boggling to me.

I was never allowed to have a girlfriend. To have a boyfriend was definitely off limits. It was taboo in our house on Harris Avenue.

Right at the end of the Home grounds driveway was a small carryout. They had penny candy and pop there too. Most of us went there whenever we could sneak away when the weather was good. It was fun to sneak away and go to the store.

Most of the storeowners didn't ask to see your dating pass. You just kept it just in case it was needed. You did not want to take a chance that someone would ask to see it and you did not have it on you.

When I arrived, the Dean of the boys kept making all kinds of snide remarks to me. Insinuating that I was not the type of girl nice boys dated, just the bad boys were interested in me. Then he would laugh and laugh at his own private joke.

He would make excuses to have me come up to his office. To see how I was doing or to see how my younger sisters were doing. I was too old for him. He only liked the innocent girls, who were still virgins.

He said, "We have several boys who have never had a dating pass before. They have asked for a dating pass now because of you." He said, "You know what this means don't you."

I said, "No! Not really."

He started laughing and carrying on as if I should know exactly what he was saying. I truly did not have a clue. He said, "They just want a piece of the action," and he would wink at me and be flirtatious like I should know exactly what he was getting at and that I should know exactly what he was meaning.

I did not understand what he was saying or what he was trying to insinuate.

He said, "Come on you know exactly what I mean, they just want a piece."

"A piece of what," I asked.

He says, "Don't play coy with me you know exactly what I am talking about."

I found out later on, much, much later on, what he had been talking about. (He always gave me the creeps.) I do not understand how he was allowed to be here as long as he was.

If no one complained to the authorities, which as far as I know no one complained (at least no while I was there) then the authorities would not have known these things were going on. These little innuendos were nothing compared to what I had been through before. I thought it was harmless. I did not know the authorities were interested in these types of goings on.

Norma Jean in her borrowed dress

Chapter 18

Three Special Dances

Where I came from having fun as a child or as a teenager was not in the best interest of the people in charge of us. Any social activity was tantamount to breaking the code of silence. I was never allowed to do anything or go anywhere unless it was punishment or work related. If there was a dance, I was not allowed to go. Doing anything outside of our immediate family was forbidden. I did not have friends my own age. This too was forbidden.

After school on Harris Avenue before the orphanage, I had to run to get home. We had ten minutes to do a mile, to get home, if we did not get home in the allotted time we got a beating.

So when I heard we were going to have a dance, I was excited. I was going to be allowed to go to a dance. This is something new for me.

I did know how to dance. I was pretty good at it too, or a least I thought, I was. I won dancing contests, especially the twisting contest. It was fun. I could move to the beat of the dance. I however did not know how to slow dance. I had two left feet or stepped on my partners feet or else I wanted to do the leading. I learned to dance watching American Band Stand on Saturday mornings. One thing they could not teach without a partner is how to slow dance with a partner. So I never learned how to do this.

The first dance I attended here at the Home was the Homecoming dance.

Since I was nominated and received runner up for Homecoming Queen, I received special treatment. I was in the Queen's court. We all wore special gowns. I borrowed a gown from my sister Karen. I had borrowed her prom dress.

I had written Karen, one of my older sisters who had come back to live in Columbus. I told her I needed a gown. I told her I did not have any money to buy a new gown. She brought up her gown from Columbus; it was from her senior prom. It fit perfectly. It was a beautiful gown.

The gown was a full length gown, down to the ankles, it was very pale, pale green lace. The underside of the gown was a darker green mixed through it. The top of the gown a gossamer piece of material sewed into it the full length of the gown as well, that I could also use a shawl. It was sleeveless and it was beautiful.

One of the other girls in the Home did my hair. It looked beautiful. It was all piled high on my head with bobby pins and hair spray to keep it in place. Big loops of curls everywhere, the bobby pins held each curl in place.

I felt like a queen. I did not need to be queen to feel like a queen. I had a boyfriend, so I had a date for the dance.

This was my first real dance and I was a senior. We had to have a date, because we needed a dancing partner. At least the Queen's court needed to have a date.

The Queen went out on the dance floor first. Then her court went out on the dance floor with her. It was fun. In the public school I had never been nominated for anything.

There were rumors flying around the Home that I was too new. I was too new to be nominated as Homecoming Queen. I should not be allowed to be Homecoming Queen. They said it just wasn't fair. The Queen should be someone who has been here for years, not someone who has been here mere weeks. Others said if I get nominated than they would boycott the dance and not go.

I did not get nominated.

I was not going to allow the rumors and gossip to ruin this for me. I wasn't trying to be selfish or anything I just wanted to have fun. I did feel like crying though. It was hard not to cry. I too felt the other girls nominated should get it because they had been there longer. No one asked me what I thought though. They just let the rumors fly loud enough for me to hear. I think they wanted me to hear them say I did not deserve this honor and they were right. I did not deserve it. I was too new.

I did have great fun!

The second special dance that I was allowed to go to this year was the Military Ball. Every year in the springtime there is a military ball. Everyone who is in R.O.T.C. has to go. Everyone has to be in R.O.T.C. It is a military home. So everyone went to the Military Ball.

This time I wore the same dress as I had worn to the Homecoming Dance. I could not afford another dress but this one was beautiful.

The Military Ball was even more formal than the Homecoming Dance.

The guy's wore their dress R.O.T.C. uniforms. The officers and their dates marched in under the swords. My boyfriend was an officer. The swords were raised above our heads and the guys who were opposite them raised their swords as well. The tips of the raised swords came together opposite each other to form an upside down v shape. It was like a bridge and we went under with arms linked together.

The guys were required to buy their dates a corsage. My corsage was a pale green to match my dress.

The first couples on the dance floor were the officers and their dates. My date was an officer.

I felt like a princess. All eyes were on the officers and their dates. I was in a beautiful gown. Yes! It was borrowed but it was still in great shape, it had only been worn twice before. This time I had to wear gloves. I had to get accessories to make it appear a little different.

It was fun. It was a special time. My date was an officer.

We danced for several hours. I still tried to do the leading. My date (boyfriend) was not happy about it in the least. I had never been taught how to slow dance and no one seemed too keen on teaching me.

The third dance was the Junior/Senior prom. We went on a riverboat ride on the Ohio River. It was very nice and very romantic. I bought a dress this time. We got some money to buy clothes for job interviews. I bought a dress that would double as a prom and an interview. It was pale blue and beautiful. I wore it for graduation.

My husband to this day says I still try to do the leading. I don't think so.

The Armory

Chapter 19

Military Orphanage

The Home was run like a well-oiled machine. To begin each day a whistle (steam whistle) sounded to get us up at 5:30am every morning. It was very loud. When it sounded, you did not sleep in or oversleep. It definitely woke you up. When the whistle blew, you could hear it in every direction of the Home grounds. There was no mistaking that sound. It was a very annoying very loud sound.

It sounded this early in the morning so that we had time to get dressed to be ready for school by 8am and still have time to go to the mess hall to eat. There were consequences for being late.

If you were late for the mess hall, you went without food until the next meal came. That is unless the cooks liked you or your cottage house parent had food in their cupboards for such an occasion and took pity on you. Then they would let you grab something and go. It had to be eaten before you went to your first class and you could not be late

The whistle went off for us to leave for school. Every time we changed classes, the whistle would sound again.

When it was time for lunch the whistle would sound again. When lunch was over the whistle would sound yet again and for us to head back to school, for the afternoon sessions. It went on like this day in and day out. This was the schedule for Monday through Friday. On weekends, it was a little different. We didn't go to school. The whistle did sound still for the mess hall. There was cold cereal for breakfast on Saturday's and Sunday's for the senior cottages. The main meal on Sunday was eaten at the mess hall, which was around lunchtime. Supper was eaten in the cottages. Something like cold cuts, things that did not require a lot of cooking.

Each cottage had its own kitchen.

On Sunday's, the whistle did sound for us to go to church. It sounded to go to breakfast, when we did not eat in the cottages. It also sounded for lunch. We had our own chapel and Reverend that preached every Sunday.

Every Memorial Day, we had a parade. The parade was to commemorate the death of the students who had died while living on the ground of the Home. There had been an epidemic and a lot of kids died during this time. We had a cemetery, so we would walk/march down to the cemetery all dressed in white and carried. It was beautiful. It was an elaborate ceremony. Each student placed flags on the graves. Someone played taps. It was solemn.

School was on the Home grounds too. We had an extensive school on the Home grounds.

For the girls there was home economics, cosmetology, clerical; which consisted of typing and shorthand. I learned a lot here. I received my first lessons on the typewriter, which helped me later on with computers. These courses helped me in my writing today. I can type a lot faster because of these courses.

In economics classes, there were some extensive classes in sewing and cooking. What we learned we could take with us and be able to cook meals on a budget. We took away some really good recipes that I still use today.

The brownies made from scratch using cocoa instead of bakers chocolate, are the best you have ever eaten.

⅔ cup flour

½ teaspoon baking powder

¼ teaspoon salt

⅓ cup butter or margarine

2 squares baker's chocolate; or 6 tablespoons cocoa + 2 tablespoons butter or margarine

1 cup sugar

2 beaten eggs

½ cup nuts (optional; I add chocolate chips instead)

1 teaspoon vanilla

Cream together butter, cocoa, sugar, eggs, and vanilla; Add remaining ingredients; Bake at 350 degrees for 20 minutes or until done.

Add a few chocolate chips in the mix and it is really good. Add melted fudge frosting and it is out of site. Good!

The one other recipe that I took away with me was the never fail flaky pie crust (this one is my favorite). It is really good. One cannot deviate from the directions; if you do, it will fail.

Never Fail Flaky Pie Crust

1/3 cup of Crisco (vegetable Crisco is ok)

¼ cup of water

Have both refrigerated

1 cup flour

Makes one pie shell; Do not double the recipe it works best if you do a single pie shell at a time.

Mix Crisco & flour together with a fork until it is pea sized balls or by using a pastry cutter.

Add the water 1 tablespoon at a time until it can be rolled into a ball. Finger it as little as possible because this warms the ingredients.

Press into a pie pan.

Everything must be chilled.

Home economics was in two parts. The first part was cooking. The second part was sewing. There was extensive study here as well. We learned to sew suits so that we could make a nice business wardrobe, including the lining of the suits, which is the most difficult part of making a suit or a dress. We learned how to make collars for shirts; how to make buttonholes; how to make a pattern; how to do the measuring for getting the proper fittings. It was pretty extensive training.

I had already done a lot of cooking before I got to the Home. I did not feel I needed to relearn this part of Home Economics (the cooking part). I was forced to take this part.

As a senior, they did not know where else to place me, without too much trouble to the rest of the classes, which were already in session. I was thoroughly upset. I could not stay with sewing.

The women, who taught this subject, told me all the girls needed a chance to learn to make an outfit. It would not be fair to the other girls if I got to make two outfits. Because the material was pretty costly and needed to be shared with all the girls who were taking home economics. I eventually relented, and had a good time. I did learn a lot too from both subjects.

These two women became very special to me as well over the course of my stay in the Home. When I graduated, these two teachers got together and bought me a sewing basket as a graduation present. I thought this was very sweet of them, very thoughtful and it was always special to me.

As I had said earlier, some of the girls who were extra special, who were not trouble makers, had the opportunity to run the switchboard. For this task or job they actually earned money. There was also other ways a girl could earn money. When there were banquets held at the Home for our superintendent and other people. The girls could wait on the tables and earn money and tips.

For the boys there was carpentry. There was also an auto mechanics trade school. There was welding. When the students left the Home most of them had some sort of a skill they could take with them and make a living with.

There was horticulture, which both boys and girls could take as a trade.

There was also a printing press. Which one could learn the typesetting of the printing press. They made the school newspaper (The Home Weekly) here plus a few other odd papers just to give the boys extensive experience.

There were several extensive labs here too, at the Home one was for science. There was an extensive dark room for developing pictures (a photo lab).

At one time there was a full scale farm. If one wanted to be a farmer, you could learn this as a trade as well.

They had some of the best milk made here on the grounds. It was ice cold and fresh. Never have I drunk such good tasting milk.

My favorite of all was drama. I was allowed to take drama. I paid attention to detail. In drama, especially when doing a play, or any other kind of a performance it is especially important to pay attention to detail.

When I first arrived at the Home, they were getting ready for the fall play. I was allowed to participate. As we were practicing, I would notice things that were not taken care of properly. I whispered to the girl sitting next to me, told her what was wrong, she told the drama teacher. There were several times that I saw the missed detail and told the girl sitting next to me and not the teacher. She got an A for the six weeks, I got a B, she also got to be a stage manager and I got to sit on the sidelines.

This taught me a very important lesson, don't be afraid to speak up. If you see, potential problems tell someone, no matter how small. From this time on when I saw a problem with the plays or performances, I tried to help fix these problems.

I loved drama. I loved the teacher who taught drama who was our drama couch. All the kids here at the Home loved the drama teacher.

The drama couch/teacher was loved so much there was an educational fund named after him to help students for their higher education. It was totally supported and funded by ex-orphans and their spouses. This was to help those ex-pupils and their spouses to pay for a college degree. Later on, it gave scholarships to our children as well.

It was called The Rooney Fund.

No one helped me out nearly as much as this teacher, Mr. Rooney. He gave me confidence I had never had before.

Every Sunday afternoon, weather permitting we had another parade. All the boys had to be in ROTC, because it was a military Home. The boys wore their parade dress uniform. They had to do practice maneuvers.

It was pretty neat to watch the proceedings. The precision of every step, every drill, and the maneuvers of the artillery rifles was pretty cool.

These were practice drills. The lines were precision straight lines as well.

Peter Pan

Chapter 20

Peter Pan

Peter Pan was the area designated for the youngest of the Home students who came here. There were a few students in my class, which had been here at the Home since they were four years old. They had no place else to go. Some had been here for twelve or thirteen years. Some even had parents who could not take care of them for various reasons.

The rooms here were a very sterile environment. The bedrooms were lined single beds all in a row, on each side of the room. The rooms were long and narrow. The beds looked more like cots than comfortable beds. They were small to accommodate the small students here. They had an army blanket as the covering and a pillow. It was all very plain and very simple. There weren't any of the trappings that you see in a child's bedroom. They wanted all the kids to be alike. They did not have separate rooms. They did not want it to be personalized either. It was very military in styling.

Each one of the students had a locker on the wall to store their personal belongings in. They were not allowed to display any of their personal belongings or nick-knack's anywhere in the room.

The children that were sent here this early had the house parents who were mean; or religious fanatics; or just plain abusive. They never had a chance to know what a normal loving family childhood would feel like. There were a lot of these kinds of cottage house parents here. The kids here helped each other cope. These children from the Home helped each other become normal productive citizens as well as they could. Just like at our house. We protected each other. We were only kids and we could not do much, mostly just observe, but we could listen.

The house parents of these cottages had to have come from an insane asylum. Some of them had some crazy ideas as to what is normal or what was to be allowed. It seemed like no one ever monitored the private goings on in each individual cottage.

I suppose I should not judge them all for being this way, just some of them. The cottage parent, who was allowed to leave the older girls cottage, because she could no longer control the older girls; was just a sampling of the cottage/house parents they had in Peter Pan. This same house parent was allowing the Dean of boys to come in and feel up these girls private parts at night. She became one of these cottage house parents.

What I saw personally was my youngest brother sitting in a school hall locker. I said, "Daryl come sit beside me" as I patted the bed I was sitting on to indicate where I wanted him to sit. I only wanted a private conversation with my brother. That old adage 'the walls have ears' was making me paranoid. My childhood thus far did not let me trust anyone outside of the perimeter of my siblings and sometimes not even them. I had already been shown that adults could not be trusted.

However Daryl did not move. He said, "I am happy where I am." No matter how much I tried to coach him into moving beside me he just wouldn't do it. He stayed seated in the locker. He did not tell me in so many words but he was told he had to sit in this locker, for me to visit with him. I felt bad for him. I did not know he would be punished even more for my just being there. This was just the beginning of his punishment.

Other things were told to me by other ex-orphans were what the house parents did to them.

I have been told, these same house parents applied ben-gay to every square inch of their bodies of these little ones, every square inch. If you have ever used ben-gay for a muscle relaxant for pain relief or for various reasons like arthritis pain, you know how it burns your skin. It is not fun. It turns your skin red. They did this every night just before the kids went to bed, so they slept this way every night. For this kind of treatment to happen to these little kids, I was horrified. I just could not believe it.

If you do not listen to what your house parent told you to do, they start poking fun at you and encouraging the other kids in your cottage to poke fun at you. They did not stop the kids from calling you names, even encouraged it. This is just another form of bullying, which they were allowed to get by with. This did nothing to build self-esteem. If you were already weak, this kind of treatment either, made you weaker or it made you stronger.

If the cottage house parent did not like you, you were truly in for a rough ride. If you had, older siblings that tried to make waves as in the case of Daryl this also got you into trouble.

It seemed like no one monitored the goings on in the orphanage and especially not in Peter Pan. The younger kids did not have as big a voice for objecting to the treatment, as did the older kids. The older kids were strong enough to retaliate, when they received treatment they hated.

We had a superintendent, who was a Colonial in the army he was in charge of the place but he never paid any attention as to the treatment of the kids that were in his charge. He did not pay any attention to the house parents or he would have known about the everyday goings on at the place. He would have smelled the ben-gay on the children in his charge and questioned the reasoning behind the smell, as it was he did not have a clue. As long as the adults did not bug him about the mundane things going on in the Home, it seemed like he could have cared less.

He did not want anyone to make waves. He was oblivious to the everyday goings on.

Like most of the adults at the Home he had his favorites too. The favorites could do no wrong. Those who were not a favorite or did not have a champion in one of the adults here had a very hard time.

Superintendent's House

Chapter 21

Christmas 1969

The Christmas of this year, nineteen hundred and sixty nine, was one of the worst Christmases, we had ever had as a family. The last one on Harris Avenue was the worst. This ranked right up there.

Before any of the Home kids went home to their homes the adults threw us a Christmas party. This party was fun though. It gave us a different perspective as to how different Christmas could be someplace else.

It was different than any other Christmas party I had ever been to. We started off with going Christmas caroling to all the residence who resided on the Home grounds. We went Christmas caroling all around the Home grounds; we caroled for those at the hospital;

we caroled for the superintendent of the Home. It was quite unique, this caroling. It was fun! There was hot chocolate afterward. It was a very cold wintry night. But kids do not seem to notice the cold as much as adults.

After the Christmas caroling was over we unwrapped presents. We all received things we needed, useful items as presents.

Unlike Harris Avenue, we always had plenty of food here. There was every kind of Christmas food imaginable set out on the tables. They always set a good spread of food. You did not go hungry and it was always good food too. The lighting was low so that we could all enjoy the huge Christmas tree in the mess hall that was all lighted up for this occasion. It was beautiful.

The ambience in the dining hall was great. It was decorated with lots and lots of Christmas decorations for the occasion. It was beautiful. Everyone had a great time.

Then we sat around our cottages and waited for someone to come and get us to take us to the home where we would be spending Christmas.

We all went to Columbus.

The grandma's, the aunts, uncles, brothers and sisters split us up.

We were split up in the Home.

I just do not understand why we could not be together for Christmas as always. No one ever cared before. Why do they care now? Were they just trying to put on a show? Were they just trying to make people believe they wanted to help us? If so, what were they trying to prove?

Daryl and Fred went to Jr's house for Christmas this year. Debbie, Joan and Jimmy went to Aunt Frieda's. I was left in the orphanage. Grandma Lamb came and got me later on, she had to work, she took me to her house.

It was the saddest, or one of the saddest times of my life. I thought that no one even cared enough about me to come and see me to make sure I went home. I was still afraid of Grandma Lamb at this time so I did not know what to expect from her but she came and got me. The rest of the week, I was by myself. Grandma worked second shift and during the day, she slept so it was as if Grandma was not there. I thought everyone was having fun.

My brothers, sisters, and I were allowed to spend one day together and that was in public view. No privacy what so ever! We found out years later that everyone had a miserable time. Fred and Daryl never did talk about it to anyone. But girls will be girls and whether our husbands approved or not we talked about our past and this was one of the subjects. What happened to the Christmas of nineteen hundred and sixty nine?

Originally, I was supposed to go to one of our Aunts homes. However, they were afraid I was going to teach their oldest son how to have sex. Isn't that all that kids like us have time to do, is have sex like our parents. I heard them discussing it, Grandma Baas and this aunt once. I went to see Grandma Baas at the hospital. It sickened me to hear such vulgar talk come out of their mouths. It was hard for me to visit this grandma after that.

None of these people ever came to see us at all after our dad died. Why all of a sudden did they want to see us now? They didn't care enough for us to keep us from going to the orphanage. Why take us out and take us to their home for Christmas now? What was their angle? What gratification did they get? When I say they never came to see us I cannot remember one time that this aunt had stepped one foot into our house. I was seventeen this Christmas. So what did they want? We never did figure this out unless, they wanted to put on a big show. They wanted to show everyone inside the orphanage they cared enough about us to get us out of the orphanage. Big Show! The joke was on us unfortunately. We needed to be together as a family unit. We needed to be allowed to talk and not be separated from each so that we could talk to each other without an audience.

So truly, they did us an injustice. They hurt us worse than they could ever imagine. All of us felt the hurt and rejection that much more severely.

Today just writing about this Christmas and thinking about it makes me want to cry, not out of self-pity. Cry for what could have been. They should have left us alone. They should have allowed Grandma Lamb to take us, just as before. Like grandma had always done. We could have talked to each other as before. This may have helped us, as a family unit. As it was these people were strangers, family but they were strangers to us.

For Debbie and Joan to go together it probably helped them to bond as never before. For the first time in their lives they saw a part of life they had never seen or experienced before. This Aunt had a daughter in between their ages and she must have gotten some of the best presents ever. There were several dolls, several outfits, several pairs of shoes, some of the most beautiful little nightgowns Debbie had ever seen in her young life. Joan saw some of the most beautiful doll clothes she had ever seen.

They got to watch our cousins open up each and every one of their presents. Debbie and Joan got an ugly neck scarf. They were told they were lucky they got that. They were also told they lucky they were there at all. Well this hurt them to the quick. Jimmy got a few things though because he had spent all last summer with them. But he did not much. They said, "This was one of the most miserable Christmases they had ever had." If the aunt and uncle didn't want them there then, why get them out of the Home to begin with? Why make themselves and the girls upset? Just leave us alone as before. Miserable! Miserable! Miserable!

Freddie and Daryl went to Junior's house for the week. Oh! I cannot imagine a more enjoyable time for them. I remember hearing stories about how Junior used to help the drunks tease Fred about how gullible he was. It used to make me sick. I remember all the yelling Junior and his wife used to do. They used to yell at their own kids all the time. I cannot imagine what another mouth or two to feed did. GEEZ! What a mess Junior never came to visit us either. I didn't understand. Why now? Why come to our aid? What purpose did it serve them?

The Band Shell

Chapter 22

Graduation

It is May 31, 1970. My graduation day it is a Sunday. The sun was shining. It was a gorgeous day. Great day for a graduation, it was an outdoor graduation held at the band shell. Yes! The Home even had its very own band shell for holding concerts and outdoor drama's. Most of the graduations at the Home were held here as long as the weather held.

Today is the day you say good-bye to all your newfound friends and family. No brothers and sisters would be allowed to go with me. I have to leave them behind, I am not happy about that but there isn't anything we can do. Leaving my brothers and sisters behind is one of the hardest things I have ever had to do. We have always been together, protecting each other.

What do I do now? How will I make it without them to look after?

We have to leave our friends and boyfriends behind too.

It is also the birthday of Jimmy and Joan the twins. Everyone had a present for Jimmy and Joan because it was their birthday. I did not really mind that they celebrated their birthday. I was relieved actually. This gave me time to say my good-byes to all my friends without any interruptions. Any other time I would have been upset, not today though.

Everyone came, even grandma Baas. Grandma Baas never came to anything for us kids. When there was a big showing or a big to do grandma Baas was there. She always liked to put on a good show. She wanted to make sure everyone knew she cared. She never cared before why now? Grandma Lamb came too she and Karen came together.

Jimmy and Joan turned fourteen years old today.

I wasn't quite eighteen yet, I was still seventeen. I was not an adult yet. Of course I was treated as an adult. I just did not have any of the adult perks.

Here in the Home the rule was if you turned eighteen before your senior year, you had to ask for permission to stay and continue going to school for your senior year. It was up to the administration, teachers, and the adults in charge, as to who was allowed to stay. Most of the students were not denied. They were allowed to stay in the Home for their senior year. I cannot remember hearing that anyone was denied, except maybe a trouble maker or two.

On graduation day, we had to be gone off the Home grounds by five o'clock. All the graduating seniors had to leave. Lock stock and barrel. You could not leave anything behind. Most of us left something special behind for our loved ones or friends we were close to. The administration didn't care if you had a place to go or not. . If they did they didn't show it. You had to make your own way now.

There was a saying eighteen, graduation and out the door whichever came first. The administration gave us a week to find a place to stay and to find a job, about two weeks before graduation day. It was up to us to make it happen.

There was one girl in my class who did not get a job, and didn't have a place to go, she still had to leave. She was a black girl, it was hard for black girls to get jobs and apartments back then. We all felt bad for her. You feel like family here skin color did not matter. Most of the rest of us had someone to go to or somewhere to go.

It was a very sad day indeed! People were crying all over the place. Some of these kids had been here since they were four years old. It was all they knew. Now what would happen to them this is all they knew?

These kids only knew the Home's whistle would wake them up. Get them off to school. Get them to the chow hall on time. Now what do you do?

The whistle blew to send us on our way! At 5:00 pm sharp, day of graduation the whistle blew just like it had for years and we all had to say our final good-byes.

Chapel

Chapter 23

After The Home

Eight and a half months after I went to the Home, I went back to live at Grandma Lamb's house. I did not know what else to do. Grandma Lamb had always taken us in even if we didn't deserve it. She did not know how to say no to us. So! Each one of us at one time or another always seemed to be moving in with her.

Two weeks after graduation I turned eighteen; I got my driver's license. Well! I tried to. The first time the car flunked. The second time I flunked. The car I was driving was a tank, well not actually. But, it felt like one. It was a big old Pontiac; the car did not have power steering. We had to parallel park the car when I first learned how to drive. If you could not parallel park you did not get your driver's license. The third time out I did get my license.

My oldest brother who was very strong from many years as a mechanic, could not even parallel park the car he had loaned me. So he found me a small compact car (hard to do back than) with powering steering and I finally passed the driving test. I was never so happy.

I went back to work for Lazarus. I worked there before I went to the Home. When I left, they told me I could come back anytime. I was hired on as a sales clerk this time. I had fun as usual. I was still a teenager and the youngest person in the department. I sold men's suits. The older men liked it too. I was a young, innocent girl who blushed a lot.

I got a ten percent discount on all my clothes. I needed clothes to be a sales clerk. So I spent some money on clothes.

I spent one year with Grandma Lamb. Grandma and I never did get along very well. I moved in with Karen who was still living in Columbus.

Karen had two children now. She was working. I helped her out by helping to babysit when time allowed. This helped to pay for my rent. Therefore, it worked out well for both of us.

I had a forty-hour workweek but I did not make that much money.

Epilog

Abuse has always been a problem in our family and still is today, as I am sure it is in a lot of families. I have written these memories down so that someone may see a child or an adult in distress and come to their aide.

Just tread carefully, that the abuser does not see. For the one being abused it will be worse if the abuser sees.

I am hoping by opening up these old wounds in our family there will be a kind of peace or healing of some sort.

May God grant us this peace!

If you know of someone who is a victim of child abuse, contact the authorities. If you know of someone, who is a victim of domestic violence also contact the authorities or at least help them get the help they need.

So be prepared for the final book in the saga.

Look for Book 5 coming out in the fall

Art's Garage

In book 5 I go in depth into my dad and his alcoholism! What did it do to his body and his mind? My poor brothers had to live with this day in and day out, their only relief was in school.

As I write all these things down there have been some really good people in my life. Before the Home there was my Sunday School teacher. Then there was a social studies teacher who gave me private speed reading courses.

In the Home there was Mr. Rooney and Mrs. Henson. I loved them all for giving me a chance. They cared enough about me to take the time to teach me.

Thank you all, for your kind words and for helping me through an otherwise bleak childhood.

The Cemetery

The Chow Hall

Roosevelt Hall (Senior Boys)

Made in the USA
San Bernardino, CA
29 May 2014